C0-BWX-798

Local Jails

Local Jails

The New Correctional Dilemma

Billy L. Wayson
Correctional Economics Center

Gail S. Funke
Correctional Economics Center

Sally F. Familton

Peter B. Meyer
The Pennsylvania State University

Lexington Books
D.C. Heath and Company
Lexington, Massachusetts
Toronto

Soc
HV
9471
L6

Robert Manning Strozier Library

NOV 4 1977

Tallahassee, Florida

Library of Congress Cataloging in Publication Data

Main entry under title:
    Local jails.

    Bibliography: p.
    Includes index.
    1. Prisons—United States. 2. Prisons—Standards—Costs—United States.
I. Wayson, Billy L.
HV9471.L6   365'.3   76-55885
ISBN 9-669-00987-3

Copyright © 1977 by D.C. Heath and Company.

All rights reserved. No part of this publication may be reproduced or transmitted in any form or by any means, electronic or mechanical, including photocopy, recording, or any information storage or retrieval system, without permission in writing from the publisher.

Published simultaneously in Canada.

Printed in the United States of America.

International Standard Book Number: 0-669-00987-3

Library of Congress Catalog Card Number: 76-55885

To the modern-day Icarus, may your wings lift you from the Labyrinth and rays of hope save you from a more ignoble end.

Contents

List of Tables

Preface

reform (ri-form'), v.t., 1. to amend or improve by change of form. 2. to make better by removing defects, malpractices, abuses and faults. . . .

This book is an exploration of reform, both of conditions and of ideas. It perhaps is fitting that it addresses our most beleaguered criminal justice entity. Amidst appeals for reform, improvement, and humane conditions, there is little questioning of its very existence. Why the jail? Why the impetus to reform an institution whose purpose and function still remain largely undefined?

In these pages we present an analysis of the economic implications of introducing jail reform through the promulgation of standards. For those seeking to go further we provide suggestions. But, just as important is a historical survey of the plight of the jail, its pivotal role in the criminal justice system, and some expressed pessimism about the prospects for defining or changing that role. What hope there is rests with a total questioning and critical assessment of criminal justice's most neglected stepchild.

The operating agency data and analysis appearing in Part II are derived from a study of jail standards compliance undertaken by the Correctional Economics Center of the American Bar Association's Commission on Correctional Facilities and Services. The conclusions are solely those of the authors who also performed the original study.

Part I

1

The Jail: Its Emergence and Contemporary Function

Many writers have chronicled the origins, development, and condition of the local jail in America and England.[1] More from a sense of necessity than tradition, however, we present a summary here to provide an understanding of problems and issues that have once again moved to the fore in the social reformers' conscience. It should not be surprising that a social institution of eight centuries' standing has remained impervious to the reformers' pleas for amelioration. Yet the shock value remains when one hears the same litany of injustices, inhuman conditions, and political paradoxes.

The jail of today had its antecedents in the eighteenth-century house of detention, the colonial gaol, and the debtors' prisons of Elizabethan England. Created during the reign of England's King Henry II (1154-1189),[2] the jail passively evolved its modern characteristics largely as a result of legal and penal reform movements aimed at changing conditions in other arenas. The original detention purpose was modified over the years so that pretrial and adjudicated persons were housed together in local jails by the thirteenth century. It took the breakup of feudal society and the resultant flood of vagabonds, vagrants, and untrained youth before Parliament in its Book of Orders of 1630-1631 required houses of corrections to be built adjacent to the local jail for petty offenders; the workhouses became residences for the less recalcitrant unemployed.

The county sheriff and justice of the peace were responsible for building and maintaining jails in England during the 1500s. Grand juries were given the duties of inspecting jails and reporting conditions to a Court of Quarter Sessions but seldom carried them out to any avail. The sheriff typically contracted, at no salary, with a keeper, because all privileges, amenities, and life's necessities were offered only on a fee-for-service basis—paid by the prisoner from personal funds, friends' donations, or begging. The schedule of payments under this much criticized fee system was not uniform (even within a shire) but varied with the dreadfulness of the offense and the prisoner's social station. Beds, mattresses, bedclothes, food, liquor, and other basics were each assigned a price; more striking, however, were the charges for admission to the jail and discharge (even if the prisoner was acquitted). In Colonial Virginia, which chose not to reject the mother country's jail traditions, the price of entry was ten pounds of tobacco, as it was for release, with an interim charge of five pounds per day.[3] The consumer-oriented model created a lucrative occupation for the keepers, who bought and sold their positions at the expense of the poor law violator. Stop

An order issued in Boston during 1632 directed that a "people pen" be constructed,[4] but it was the General Assembly of Virginia that first created the basic administrative pattern that still characterizes the nation's jails. The six shires (counties) of Virginia were directed in 1842 to construct jails for the detention of prisoners awaiting monthly sessions of General Court in Jamestown.[5] The legislation that called for these jails also established what were probably the first multijurisdictional jail standards by prescribing the construction materials (timber) and security devices (iron grate) to be used. Recognizing the deterrent effects of potential sanctions, the assembly established penalties for noncompliance and required damage payments from local counties for harm perpetrated by escapees. This model, which was borrowed from England, marked the beginning of a trend that would be followed for the next three hundred years.

The New Amsterdam jail-prison (1642) and the well-known workhouse erected by the Philadelphia Quakers in 1682[6] represented minor variations of the general concept. The General Court and Assembly of the Massachusetts Bay Colony, however, adopted the Virginia model and voted in 1669 to add county prisons to the sheriff's purview.[7] Almost one hundred years later (1785), the Massachusetts General Court ordered the construction of jails in every town that hosted judicial proceedings.[8]

Public outrage and official condemnation have been as much a part of jails as locks, grills, pillories, and stocks. "In regard to our county prisons," wrote the Reverend Dwight in 1831, "nothing has been done in the way of reform."[9] America's jails were the subject of discussion at the 1870 National Congress of Penitentiary and Reformatory Discipline[10] and rose to world notoriety at the Eighth International Prison Congress in the early years of this century. Sir Evelyn Ruggles-Brise found a "startling inconsistency" between progressive penal reform in this country and persistent conditions in "common goals." They were a blight that made it "impossible for America to have assigned to her by general consent a place in the vanguard of progress in the domain of 'la science penitentiare.' "[11] The foreign delegates had found during their inspections unsanitary conditions, idleness, corruption, a modified fee system, the insane, and long periods of pretrial detention. The nation's penologists were not blind to the problem but, if anything, were more strident: the stalwart reformer, E.C. Wines, warned the National Conference of Charities and Corrections (1911) that the only hope was "overthrow of the county jail system."[12] Only the state could "find a way to right the wrong and remedy the evils which inhere in the present organization and management of minor prisons"—heralding a theme to be echoed for decades. Indeed, the literature of the times suggests that castigating jails was a popular pasttime.[13]

After touring many jails and reviewing state reports, Robinson concluded that jails in 1923 remained much as they had been for centuries, in spite of increased probation, installment fines, and fewer juveniles.[14] An even more systematic analysis of prevailing conditions came during the ensuing years from inspectors of the Federal Bureau of Prisons, which was responsible for the supervision of detainees awaiting trial in federal courts. The bureau surveyed three thousand local jails in 1938; almost 65 percent (1944) were totally unfit to house federal prisoners and 480 were suitable for emergency use only.[15] Even then conditions were far from any pragmatic ideal, because over 96 percent were in compliance with less than 60 percent of the bureau's standards.

The modern reformer who places trust in the efficacy of prestigious study groups or national gatherings of renowned professionals to spark change should remember the National Commission of Law Observance and Enforcement chaired by Wickersham. An advisory report to the commission called local jails "dirty, unhealthy, unsanitary—and ill-fitted to produce either a stabilizing or beneficial effect on inmates."[16] Following their British colleagues, the advisory committee labeled the American jail the "most notorious correctional institution in the world."[17] A few years later, a speaker informed the Attorney General's Conference on Crime (1934) that conditions were "so medieval, and barbarous, and so contrary to the ordinary tenets of democracy and social justice that [he] was shocked beyond expression."[18] He recovered sufficiently to convince the conference that it should resolve to "specifically condemn the unsafe, insanitary and insecure conditions which exist in many local jails throughout the country."[19]

Traditions—the jail and its detractors—change slowly, so three decades later the plight of the local jails again was officially certified.

Not only are the great majority of these facilities old, but many do not even meet the minimum standards in sanitation, living space, and segregation of different ages and types of offenders that have obtained generally in the rest of corrections for several decades.[20]

Not to be outdone, the Corrections Task Force of the National Advisory Commission on Criminal Justice Standards and Goals was less equivocal and painted with broader strokes: "Outmoded and archaic, lacking the most basic comfort, totally inadequate for any program encouraging socialization, jails perpetuate a destructive rather than reintegrative process."[21]

The knowledge base for early reformers was largely limited to personal observations or, at best, to reports from specific states. Only recently has anyone begun to collect statistics that describe the local jail in a regular and systematic way.

In mid-1972, there were an estimated 3921 jails holding about 142,000 prisoners for forty-eight hours or more.[22] Their more salient features were:

1. Employees—44,298, or one for each 3.2 inmates.
2. Location—61 percent were in a police, sheriff's, or court building; 34 percent were separate.

3. Population—Only 36 percent separated pretrial from sentenced prisoners; 18 percent housed work-releasees separately
4. Meals—Two-thirds provided three meals, but 59 percent served them in cells
5. Health care—only 480 (12 percent) had medical facilities
6. Recreation—16 percent had recreation yards
7. Programs—42 percent had work-release programs, but only 825 (21 percent) operated other programs on their own

Although these statistics might not surprise those with a historical understanding or experience in jail operations, they reinforce long-held beliefs. There are exceptions, variations, and explanations, but the statistics confirm general conditions in jails nationwide.

If documentation of jail conditions is notable for its repetitiveness, assessment of causes only adds to the din. Contemporary writers have cited obsolete facilities, too many prisoners, lack of money, untrained employees, and political patronage.[23] These conditions, however, historically have been deemed only symptomatic of the first cause—the large number and small size of local jails. The National Congress on Penitentiary and Reformatory Discipline, the Wickersham Commission, the Attorney General's Conference, the President's Crime Commission, and a host of other private reformers and public bodies have expressed a sense of being overwhelmed by the simple numbers.[24] Baseline standards of housing, medical care, feeding, and so on are (were) generally agreed upon, but meeting them seems to require more resources than any one (or even several) political subdivisions can or will commit.

If defining a problem is half its solution, the recurring catalog of ills implies a parallel history for the palliatives. For the past two hundred years, the general strategy has been reactionary—returning the jail to its original purpose of pretrial detention. True, the proposed means sometimes involved shifts in responsibilities or a different population or more humane conditions; the *purpose*, however, was to recreate a less deleterious jail to hold persons awaiting an appearance before a judicial officer. The means to this end have varied only slightly and involved either changes in population (type, intake, or outflow) or intervention by more general units of government (regional, state, or federal); even though, a variety of techniques have been recommended to alter the jail's clientele or its administrative structure.

A recurring theme in the history of these institutions is the changing populations they housed. The jail gave way to the workhouse and house of corrections in mid-sixteenth-century England as growing unemployment and poverty forced the search for alternatives; fines and corporal punishment made the local jail a place for those awaiting trial. Legal reform in the eighteenth century reduced the number of crimes carrying capital sanctions, created the longer sentence, and spawned state prisons. Orphans and debtors, however, still filled American jails through the first half of the 1800s. The Prison Discipline

Society of Boston reported (1831) that in states surveyed by its secretary, Reverend Louis Dwight, there were three to five debtors for every "regular" prisoner in county jails.[25] The orphan asylum and house of refuge siphoned off not only delinquents but also poor children from local jails between 1830 and 1860.[26] Over 80 percent of the states had established institutions for the insane by 1860,[27] further lessening the strain on local jails to serve a multitude of ends for the delinquent, homeless, poor, unemployed, and feeble-minded. The ills of that aged institution remained, however.

The insane asylum, orphanage, penitentiary, and reformatory removed whole classes of offenders from the jails. Then there were attempts to alter the processing of those who remain. Pretrial alternatives are a common way of reducing intake, and "perhaps the first step toward reform would be to find ways to avoid committing people to local jails."[28] Percentage or low bail and release on recognizance at the arraignment stage in the criminal justice process have been used to varying degrees for many years. Only recently, however, have methods for assuring appearance at trial—other than physical custody—demonstrated their effectiveness and gained wide acceptance. The use of field citations and summons in lieu of arrest for minor offenses, such as traffic violations, has increased. Pretrial diversion—where proceedings are held in abeyance pending successful completion of a specific program—has become common since the midsixties but may not be, in fact, used extensively; for example, the American Bar Association Commission on Correctional Facilities and Services listed only 118 such projects in 1975. With all of these attempts to reduce the number of prisoners awaiting trial, there is some question as to whether or not they simply expand the criminal justice net by placing under control persons who would have been released in any event. These practices, combined with alternative sentencing dispositions (installment fines, misdemeanant probation, weekend sentences) may have an even more profound effect on the jail, its population, management, and operation. Screening out low-risk, less serious offenders at the pretrial stage and choosing noninstitutional alternatives for persons who typically would have served only a 30- or 60-day sentence very likely will increase the average length of stay for both sentenced and unsentenced prisoners! This situation may be further exacerbated by trends toward harsher misdemeanant penalties generally (that is, 90 days becomes 180 days) and overcrowding in state institutions, which delays transfer of sentenced felons. The net effect is that the jail, as it has so many times in history, contains a population that it is ill-suited and ill-prepared to house, either by design or experience. If cells, recreation space, and visiting rooms were substandard for a relatively short-term group, they are even worse for persons who may be incarcerated for six to twelve months. If operations and programs are structured to accommodate a turnover of 1000 percent annually, they cannot readily adjust to deal with the monotony, isolation, violence, and other debilitating conditions that result from incarceration with minimal supervision in dormitories, four-person cells, and comingling. Although the effect of pretrial and sentencing alternatives can be documented for individual jails (for example, King County, Washington), time series data is too new to allow conclusions on a national scale. However, if there is a trend away from incarceration—and it should be closely monitored—it may represent one of the most significant developments in local incarceration since the advent of state penitentiaries. The difference lies in the fact that now the forces creating the conditions are much more subtle and diffuse and originate from changes in judicial procedures, law enforcement operations, prosecutorial decisions, correctional agency practices and general public concern for reducing crime through harsher penalties. This diversity will make it more difficult to effect jail improvement, irrespective of what action government takes.

Varying degrees of state intervention—from total control to oversight and standards setting—have been suggested repeatedly as a general reform strategy. An advocate of state-operated regional facilities for misdemeanants at the 1870 corrections conference emphasized that they would relieve local jails of sentenced prisoners.[29] They cited the growing number of minor offenses, brutalities at the county level, and draconian consequences of penitentiary imprisonment as reasons to adopt this intermediate "district house of discipline." Gubernatorial appointments to a local board of trustees could then oversee the improvement of a less crowded jail. Believing that opposition to state control originated from a "very selfish wish to benefit special interests deriving a profit from the local institution," Robinson pointed to an alternative in southern states, where jail prisoners repaired roads under state supervision.[30] The Advisory Committee to Wickersham was probably the first to officially suggest a range of functions that would be appropriately performed by state government. Besides establishing "industrial farm colonies" for sentenced misdemeanants, states should have authority to set standards covering food, sanitation, living conditions, and so on; inspect facilities for compliance; approve construction plans; close substandard jails; transfer, at county expense, prisoners in the interest of community and prisoner welfare.[31] The Crime Commission (1967) and the Standards and Goals Commission (1973) went further and recommended state operation under a corrections agency, with prescriptive standards only as a second-best solution.[32]

The search for someone or something to reform the local jail did not exclude the federal government. Legislation authorizing federal inspections was an outgrowth of the Attorney General's Conference in 1934. Much earlier, the Treasury was seen as a possible source of support. A Key West, Florida, grand jury requested a federal appropriation for construction in 1829 and two years later received authorization to retain $2000 from the territorial tax on auction sales to build a jail and dig one cistern.[33] The precedent for this action was the ten thousand acres donated to rebuild the Detroit jail, which had burned in 1805. In 1925 one federal judge went so far as to suggest that federally-operated jails for prisoners of the U.S. government "could stand as examples to which states might make their jails conform."[34] During the depression era, substantial amounts of federal dollars, in fact, did flow into jail construction. Through June 1941 the Works Progress Administration funded 156 new prison buildings, 482 remodelings, and 32 additions, some of which undoubtedly were jails.[35] Other agencies contributed to 186 new facilities, either as separate units or part of court houses. In April 1976 the U.S. Comptroller General recommended two approaches, other than direct funding, in a report to Congress: first, the Justice Department and states should jointly set standards that jails must meet in order to receive Federal dollars for physical improvements, and, second, funding should be contingent upon a plan for attaining compliance with minimum standards.[36]

Standards-setting is a less drastic intervention which can be traced to the earliest periods of this country's history. By 1807, laws in Alabama required that jails be secured by timber, grates, bolts, and locks, and supplemented with pillories, whipping posts and stocks.[37] Mississippi required (1822) stronger fortifications of stone or brick.[38] State regulations encompassed feeding, reimbursement schedules for sheriffs, and even the distribution of Bibles, but, as one writer concluded, "jails seldom, if ever, met criteria established by statute."[39] Nonetheless, public policy continued to focus on jail standards until almost 70 percent of the states had passed some form of standards-setting legislation by mid-1974; thirty-four states had some form of state inspection, but less than one-half (21) included enforcement powers.[40] The Standards and Goals Commission, noting the persistence of adverse conditions, recommended "a system of state inspection, with effective procedures for enforcement"[41] only as an interim step to state control. Standard 9.3, "inspection of local facilities," even recommended that the regulatory agency have condemnation authority, if local governments did not implement necessary changes.[42]

In general, the trend over the last twenty years has been toward some form of state intervention through standards-setting, jail inspection, and/or enforcement. Some statutes directly incorporate substantive standards; others assign promulgation to an administrative body or executive agency. Enforcement powers range from nonexistent to outright authority to close facilities or seek judicial remedies.[43] More recent recommendations have varied dramatically from this trend by calling for total state control and integration with a broader correctional system. Concomitantly, there have been untireless efforts to alter the type or number of persons incarcerated at the local level. Debtors, mentally ill, vagrants, juveniles, alcoholics, and other deviants from current social norms, for the most part, have been channeled to alternative (if not better) situations. Despite these efforts, the local jail, regardless of its condition, remains "a place of first or last resort for a host of disguised welfare and social problem cases."[44]

Whether motivated by humanitarian concern, judicial decrees, political pressure, operational problems, local parsimony, or some combination of these, there appears to be a renewed national interest and concern for ameliorating local jail conditions. A common approach to social problems historically has been to abdicate responsibility to ever higher levels of government. It is doubtful, however, that such a tack is possible with jails, if for no other reason than sheer numbers. Jails have tenaciously resisted improvement (albeit not passive change), because no single unit or branch of government has the resources to fundamentally alter the purpose, organization, management, and operation of local detention facilities, even if the political resolve could be summoned. Within a single jurisdiction, the solution is further complicated by the fact that powerful interest groups—judiciary, law enforcement, state corrections, local elected officials—are part of the problem and, hence, must contribute to the solution. After eight centuries, the central issues and questions remain. Are judges willing to adopt alternatives to pretrial detention? Will sheriffs surrender control to professionally trained managers? Can county commissioners publicly assign a high priority to the socially ostracized? Is it reasonable for state corrections to openly acknowledge that their "supply" originates at the local level? It may be, as it was 65 years ago, that "[t]he political forces and interests which favor retention of the system cannot for the present be overcome."[4][5] The issues associated with the local jail are much the same today, irrespective of past political actions.

A thorough analysis of all jail-related issues should include a discussion of the many alternatives to jail incarceration at the pretrial stage (citation, summons, ROR, diversion) and at the sentencing stage (misdemeanant probation, weekend sentences, alcohol rehabilitation, restitution), as well as an examination of the effects of speedy trials, overcrowding in state institutions, law enforcement efforts, and prosecutorial priorities. Such completeness must await another book.

The overriding policy question surrounding the concept of standards is their efficacy in guiding local action toward desired ends. As too frequently happens with social policy, practice preceded theory without a thorough examination of what approaches held the best prospect for upgrading and without a precise statement of what standards were intended to achieve. It is now conventional wisdom that some degree of centralization within a framework of mutually agreeable operating norms will produce institutions that treat people with basic human decency.

A historical perspective, if nothing else, should disabuse the well-intentioned reformer of the illusion that standards by themselves will significantly alter the state of affairs. Indeed, there are economic, legal, and other legitimate obstacles to change in this field, but in the final analysis it becomes a question of political trade-offs, relative power, and courage. Unlike other recipients of the government's beneficence, the clientele do not vote; the citizens who do vote have little concern for conditions in their local jail and, in fact, probably consider them a "just dessert." It seems appropriate now, at a time when expressions of official concern with the plight of jails are more frequent than in the past, to reflect for the first time on whether centralization and standards point to reform or simply to retrenchment of the status quo. Here we will limit ourselves to questions surrounding standards and consolidation: the first because it is one form of state intervention, short of outright control, that has many proponents; the second because some see larger jails as a solution to the problem of meeting minimum standards at an acceptable unit cost and a likely consequence of aggressive state action.

↙ Experiences in many states clearly demonstrate that setting jail standards is a complex, time-consuming, and sometimes costly process. Given the nationally recognized need to improve local facilities and programs, however, many have advocated it as the principal strategy for altering an institution that processes 1 to 2 million persons annually in an atmosphere of conflicting purposes and public apathy. Approaches to developing standards vary, but the commission or similar body representing varying interests is common to many jurisdictions. The organization's structure, membership, staff support, and interaction with related agencies are key factors to consider in establishing such a body.

Once a commission has been established, whether by the legislature or administratively, representation becomes an important issue. The pivotal role of the jail, not only in the criminal justice system but also in the local community, makes changes in its operation a concern to many different private citizens, public officials, and interest groups. A local jail serves important law enforcement functions (booking and release), court services (pretrial detention and appearance at trial), and correctional needs (supplying offenders to state institutions, holding sentenced state prisoners, and operating some rehabilitation programs). An important consideration for the larger community may be the short-term custody for behavior it deems "undesirable," such as vagrancy, nonsupport, disputants in domestic quarrels, mental illness, and so on. These multifaceted activities require a standards commission with a broadly based functional, geographical, jurisdictional, and professional membership. Functional representation includes law enforcement officials, prosecutors, defense counsel, the judiciary, and corrections and elected officials. The level at which persons perform these functions is important: state, county, and municipal governments each have different perspectives and responsibilities. It can be helpful to include a "national," ex officio member to serve as a disinterested party and to provide information about other states' experiences. Finally, professional representation from the health, legal, social science, or other fields offers expertise in areas that will probably receive priority for implementation. Transferring responsibility and diffusing it through a committee process are convenient ways of concealing culpability for what may appear to many to be coddling.

To sustain an ongoing standards process, a part-time commission requires the staff capability not only to carry out its standards formulation activities but also to perform jail inspections and assist local jail officials in implementation. Jails and criminal justice, generally, are in a constant state of flux, so today's standards can become tomorrow's unacceptable performance. To assure continued relevance, the commission through its staff must:

1. Identify emerging needs, such as managing drug addicts.
2. Monitor trends in population flows.
3. Isolate changes in the demographic characteristics of jail populations.
4. Prepare documents that can be used by the commission in its deliberations.
5. Develop estimates of implementation costs for proposed or newly adopted standards.

Although difficult, formulating standards may be less onerous than evaluating compliance. Both commonality and uniqueness among jails must be accounted for if standards are to be equitably applied. Again, the day-to-day responsibility falls on the full-time staff. Their tasks include:

1. Developing the type of facility and program inspection instruments that will yield usable information for decisions, the actual conditions statewide, implementation progress, new standards, cost impacts, and so on. This task is complicated by the fact that different types of standards (for example, food service and health care) may require different inspection methods (for example, on-site versus document review) and different rating schemes (for example, continuous scales or simply "acceptable/unacceptable").
2. Establishing and maintaining a regular inspection schedule. A total review of each facility may not be necessary annually, but simply selected aspects deemed to be a priority or important for a specific jail's compliance.
3. Collating and reporting information from field trips in a way that contributes to making the kinds of decisions discussed above.

The proverbial "slip twixt cup and lip" frequently characterizes the step from standards promulgation to implementation. Standards compliance is dependent on resource availability, officials' preferences, the standards' relevance, citizen interest, and a host of other factors, any of which may hamper or delay jail improvement. Because the content of any set of standards varies widely, so will implementation actions. The jailer, for example, can order the preparation of a policy manual and it can be completed with minimal or zero costs in a short time. Increasing meals to three daily may require additional appropriations, which must await several months for the budget process. However, a capital improvement requires detailed study and architectural estimates even prior to budget request or a bond referendum. Legislative changes may require several years. Each of these possible implementation strategies (administrative, budgetary, and legislative) or combinations of them entail varying lead times, resources, and decision makers.

During the implementation process, it will be important to establish priorities that are cognizant of the factors mentioned above and based on whatever general criteria a deliberative body selects. If personnel, for example, are deemed a priority, then standards should be viewed in this light; health care, on the other hand, involves a set of standards with facility, equipment, and personnel costs.

Standards written during the formulation process need to be phrased so that one will know when they have been implemented, either at a particular jail or statewide. Statements of principle are important to explaining the rationale underlying a standard but do not emphasize what they are intended to accomplish. Formulating standards in language that refers as much as possible to reasonably observable events facilitates monitoring.

There is sufficient knowledge today to reach agreement on what needs to be done, but how it should be done requires substantially improved data bases and analyses. All of the duties and functions outlined above point to the critical need to improve the quality, comparability, quantity of data on annual and year-to-year population flows through local jails. One state's jail inspector reported that "statistical information is difficult to obtain regarding prisoners who were actually placed in a cell. . . . The number of bookings from those literally placed into a jail may not be reflected in the compilation of yearly statistical data. . . . Uniformity in recording and booking procedures and statistics of jail operation in the State has been recommended for some time."[46] Yet, conditions had barely improved three years later when the cognizant body requested legislative approval for its standards and an appropriation to subsidize implementation.

Even within a state, jurisdictions do not use common (or reasonably comparable) definitions of key terms. For example:

How are "average daily populations" computed? Is a count taken at 6 P.M., 12 midnight, or 6 A.M. and considered the "daily" population? Or are accumulated mandays used?

How long must an inmate be held to produce a "manday" of detention? Six, twelve, or twenty-four hours?

Aside from the gross felony/misdemeanant distinction, what offense definitions are used, if any?

Do "capacity" figures include special purpose bed space such as infirmary or isolation cells?

Comparable definitions among jails and from year to year would improve the capability to make interjurisdictional comparisons annually and to identify changes in key variables (bookings, average daily populations, offense mix, and so on) over time and monthly. It is important to distinguish between various legal statuses of persons held in local jails for both constitutional and management purposes. Turnover can have a significant impact on institutional costs and

14

operations, but computing such rates requires statistics on bookings, pretrial release, admissions, discharges, and length of time awaiting trial or transfer. It could be important for planning to know the level and changes in contracting between jurisdictions; if reimbursements are not reported in sufficient detail, it may be impossible to determine true operating costs of a jail.

We have highlighted (not exhausted) some of the simple baseline statistics necessary to make informed decisions about how jail populations are changing statewide, differences between jails, effects of change in law enforcement, court or prosecution agencies, and what seem to be emerging problems. These data either do not exist or are not centrally compiled in most cases; but it is precisely this type of information that is necessary if jurisdictions intend to rationally consider such difficult policy chores as standards promulgation, implementation subsidization, compliance monitoring, regionalization, and a host of other questions.

One of the effects attributed to local control is a proliferation of small jails that results in underutilization, lack of programs and untrained staff.[47] Table 1-1, compiled from national data, indicates that small jails have less programming, whether financed internally or externally, and that their facilities are less adequate. For example, only 10 percent of the small jails, compared to 43 percent of the large ones, have vocational training programs supported by nonfederal funds. A smaller percentage of small jails receives federal support for any program. Work-release and weekend sentences are the only categories in which small jails approach comparability with larger ones. The dilemma, of course, is that most small facilities are in locales where services are not available in the community, so even the referral option is foreclosed. In selected service or facility areas, small jails show similar deficiencies: 32 percent separate sentenced and pretrial inmates, compared to 58 percent of the large jails; 60 percent serve three meals, but almost all large jails do.

A common conclusion is that small jails are the most costly—whether relatively or absolutely is not always clear—and, therefore, larger units are justified. To be valid, however, this argument needs supporting premises or assumptions that are seldom (if ever) stated explicitly: small jails are usually located in sparsely populated, less industrially developed areas where sales, property, business, or other tax revenues are not large; the burden of financing the local jails is disproportionate; therefore, sufficient funds are not appropriated. "Small pay and little opportunity do not attract a big man,"[48] so personnel are less qualified or jail supervision is delegated to road deputies. The factors determining cost are much more complicated than this facile analysis would lead one to believe.

After examining the dilemma of how to provide basic detention services and, at the same time, maintain some level of efficiency in small jails, task forces, study groups, and funding agencies frequently recommend regional facilities for sentenced inmates and smaller, local facilities for temporary

Table 1-1
Number of Jails with Programs by Size of Jail

Programs	Total (3921)	Small (less than 21) Total–2901		Medium (21-249) Total–907		Large (250 or more) Total–113	
		n	percent	n	percent	n	percent
Federally funded	475	184	6.3	233	25.7	58	51.3
Referral to federally funded	635	394	13.6	191	21.1	50	44.2
Other funding	2646	1722	59.4	816	90.0	108	95.6
Operated from outside	2365	1580	54.5	703	77.5	82	72.6
Operated internally	825	379	13.1	359	39.6	88	77.9
Nonfederal vocational training programs	542	288	9.9	205	22.6	49	43.4
Work-related programs	1665	1182	40.7	434	47.9	49	43.4
Weekend sentences	1821	1256	43.3	498	54.9	67	59.3
Services/Facilities							
Three or more meals	2628	1747	60.2	772	85.1	109	96.5
Medical facility	480	111	3.8	270	29.8	99	87.6
Recreational facility	2422	1592	54.9	720	79.4	110	97.3
Separate pretrial/sentenced[a]	1400	940	32.4	396	43.7	65	57.5

Source: Law Enforcement Assistance Administration, *The Nation's Jails*, Tables 6-8, 11, 17-21, and 23-25.

[a]"Not applicable" or "not available" reported for 363 small, 135 medium, and 14 large jails.

detention. The National Advisory Commission on Criminal Justice Standards and Goals has given impetus to the regionalization concept:

A regionalized service delivery system should be developed for service areas that are sparsely populated and include a number of cities, towns or villages. Such a system may be city-county or multicounty.[49]

A reason frequently cited for regionalization is lower cost, and a casual examination of data may seem to support this notion. Detailed analysis, however, will sometimes show increased resource needs.[50] Consequently, "a systematic analysis of cost factors should be part of the planning process and be included in the overall cost projections."[51] The reasonableness of consolidation depends on the objectives set for each facility; population flows between different parts of the criminal justice system; the proportion of inmates in pretrial presentencing, felon, and misdemeanant statuses; geographical distance; optimum scale of plant; and many other cost- and noncost-related variables. A facility, however costly, may provide services that the community feels are important. If services (unavailable from any other source) are provided locally to releasees from state institutions, the high-cost institution may be the only solution under the conditions. A large, consolidated facility, perhaps, can offer more programs and thereby accommodate persons who otherwise would have been sent to state institutions. If speedier trials are a goal in a jurisdiction, transfers of even twenty miles may result in higher total costs than maintaining an apparently inefficient jail. Even if other factors show that consolidation is less costly, there remains the question of optimum plant size.

The national average population was 36 inmates per facility in 1972, but 74 percent of the 3921 jails holding prisoners longer than forty-eight hours accommodated 20 or fewer prisoners; only 3 percent housed 250 or more.[52] Although averages have increased over the 1923 census estimates of 11 or less,[53] the majority of jails are probably too small even to approach economic efficiency. Within the gross range between 20 and 250, the unanswered question remains the optimum scale from an economic, rehabilitative, and social point of view. The large jail may be most efficient from a narrow cost perspective, but suboptimal in light of the psychological and sociological effects of congregate living. Or a large facility built for efficiency reasons may end up housing persons who would be better served in the community at a lower social cost. Unit costs depend on quantity produced, factor prices, and quality of the "output," but both quality and quantity are difficult to define for correctional organizations. Studies focusing only on the economic questions have not been conclusive. For example, one study[54] of 35 California jails produced both linear and nonlinear capital cost functions with equal and very low explanatory power. The linear form implied that investment per inmate continually declined; the nonlinear that the optimum size was 26 in terms of capital cost only. Sample size restricted interpretation of results using operating costs. A capacity of 49 would minimize operating costs per bed, according to another study of 51 Indiana jails,[55] but the author did not include an allowance for capital cost. The most economically efficient scale for local institutions is unknown, to say nothing of less precise effects of size. Nevertheless, lack of knowledge has not been an obstacle to making recommendations for regional facilities or consolidation and basing them on simple average-unit-cost comparisons. The question of consolidation is much more complex and, as yet, unanswered objectively.

Jail standards have a long tradition in the United States but the last 20 years has witnessed their proliferation. They usually have been advocated as the primary way of spurring improvement in deplorable conditions that have been documented for 150 years. Confronted with persistent local inaction or inability, larger regional facilities are suggested as a way of spreading costs among jurisdictions and, thereby, making standards compliance possible. Although centralization through mandated standards and consolidation has become popular, the most basic policy question regarding the efficacy of this approach remains woefully unanswered. Logic, however, is not the foundation of faddish panaceas, so we are likely to see expanded involvement by state and federal governments, wide use of subsidies to motivate implementation, and recurring conflicts over the real need for more bricks and the best methods of operation. If this is the tack, hopefully the process will be more systematic and thoughtful than the sporadic flailings of earlier, sincerely motivated reformers. Among other things, this style will require a better articulated rationale for the necessity of standards, and the ends to be achieved by them, difficult and sometimes unpopular choices of priorities, and judicious allocation of scarce resources.

Notes

1. Besides those cited later, these include Sidney and Beatrice Webb, *English Prisons Under Local Government* (Hamden, Conn.: Shoe String Press, 1963); Michael Dalton, *County Justice* (London: John Walthoe, 1715); Joseph Fishman, *Crucibles of Crime* (New York: Cosmopolis Press, 1923); Frank Hoffer, Delbert Martin, and Floyd House, *The Jails of Virginia* (New York: Appleton-Century, 1933).

2. Louis Robinson, *Penology in the United States* (Philadelphia: J.C. Winston, 1923), p. 33 (hereafter *Penology*). See Henry Burns, Jr., *Origin and Development of Jails in America* (Carbondale, Ill.: Center for the Study of Crime and Delinquency, n.d.) for a summary of the history of jails (hereafter *Jails in America*).

3. Burns, *Jails in America*, p. 8.

4. P.D. Jordan, "The Close and Stinking Jail," *Frontier Law and Order: Ten Essays* (Lincoln, Neb.: University of Nebraska Press, 1970), p. 140 (hereafter "The Close and Stinking Jail").

5. Burns, *Jails in America*, p. 9.

6. Jordan, "The Close and Stinking Jail," pp. 140-141.

7. Robinson, *Penology*, pp. 36-37.

8. Jordan, "The Close and Stinking Jail," p. 140.

9. Orlando F. Lewis, *The Development of American Prisons and Prison Customs, 1776-1845* (Montclair, N.J.: Patterson Smith, 1967), Reprint Series in Criminology, Law Enforcement and Social Problems, no. 1, p. 278 (hereafter *American Prisons and Prison Customs*).

10. A.G. Byers, "District Prisons Under State Control for Persons Convicted of Minor Offenses: Size, Organization and Discipline Suited to Them," *Transactions of the National Congress on Penitentiary and Reformatory Discipline*, E.C. Wines, ed. (Albany: Weed, Parsons, 1871; reprinted by American Correctional Association, 1970), pp. 219-231 (hereafter *Transactions*).

11. Sir Evelyn Ruggles-Brise, "English View of the American Penal System," *Journal of the American Institute of Criminal Law and Criminology*, vol. 2, no. 3 (September 1911), p. 366, quoted in Robinson, *Penology*, n. 2, p. 41 (hereafter "American Penal System").

12. Lewis, *American Prisons and Prison Customs*, p. 269.

13. See Edith Abbot, *The One Hundred and One County Jails of Illinois and Why They Ought to Be Abolished* (Chicago: Juvenile Protective Association of Chicago, 1916); H. Francis Spencer, *Confessions of a Jailer* (Long Beach, Calif.: H. Francis Spencer, 1914); Oscar Dowling, "The Hygiene of Jails, Lock-ups and Police Stations," *Journal of the American Institute of Criminal Law and Criminology* vol. 5 (January 1915); Winthrop Lane, "Uncle Sam, Jailer: A Study of the Conditions of Federal Prisoners in Kansas Jails," *Survey*, vol. 42 (1919); and Joseph Fishman, "The American Jail: Pages from the Diary of a Prison Inspector," *Atlantic Monthly*, vol. 130 (December 1922).

14. Robinson, *Penology*, pp. 29-44.

15. Louis N. Robinson, *Jails: Care and Treatment of Misdemeanant Prisoners in the United States* (Philadelphia: J.D. Winston, 1944), p. 10 (hereafter, *Jails*).

16. National Commission on Law Observance and Enforcement, *Report on Penal Institutions, Probation and Parole*, Report of the Advisory Committee on Penal Institutions, Probation and Parole (Washington, D.C.: Government Printing Office, 1931), p. 272 (hereafter, National Commission).

17. Ibid., p. 273.

18. Joseph C. Hutcheson, "The Local Jail," *Proceedings of the Attorney General's Conference on Crime, December 10-13*, 1934 (Washington, D.C., n.d.), p. 233 (hereafter "Local Jail").

19. Ibid., p. 454.

20. U.S. President's Commission on Law Enforcement and the Administration of Justice, *Task Force Report: Corrections* (Washington, D.C.: Government Printing Office, 1967), p. 75 (hereafter, President's Commission).

21. National Advisory Commission on Criminal Justice Standards and Goals, *Corrections* (Washington, D.C.: Government Printing Office, 1973), p. 309 (hereafter Standards and Goals Commission).

22. U.S. Department of Justice, Law Enforcement Assistance Administration, *The Nation's Jails* (Washington, D.C.: Government Printing Office, 1975), p. 1. The statistics that follow are also drawn from this source (hereafter, *Nation's Jails*).

23. Hans W. Mattick and Alexander B. Aikman, "The Cloacal Region of American Corrections," *The Annals of the American Academy of Political and Social Science*, no. 381 (January 1969), p. 110 (hereafter "Cloacal Region"). A similar list for one state is given in Gary Stracensky et al., *Texas Jails—Problems*

and Reformation, Criminal Justice Monograph, vol. III, no. 4 (Huntsville, Tex.: Institute of Contemporary Corrections and Behavioral Science, 1971).

24. See Robinson, *Penology*, pp. 44-46; Byers, op. cit., p. 220; National Commission, p. 275; President's Commission, p. 75.

25. Lewis, *American Prisons and Prison Customs*, p. 277.

26. David Rothman, *The Discovery of the Asylum: Social Order and Disorder in the New Republic* (Boston: Little, Brown, 1971), pp. 207-208 (hereafter *Asylum*).

27. Ibid., p. 130.

28. Mattick and Aikman, "Cloacal Region," p. 111.

29. Byers, *Transactions*, pp. 219-231.

30. Robinson, *Penology*, pp. 48-50.

31. National Commission, p. 278.

32. President's Commission, p. 80; Standards and Goals Commission, pp. 292-295.

33. Jordan, "The Close and Stinking Jail," p. 142.

34. Hutcheson, "Local Jail," p. 227.

35. Robinson, *Jails*, p. 170.

36. U.S. Comptroller General, *Conditions in Local Jails Remain Inadequate Despite Federal Funding Improvements* (Washington, D.C.: General Accounting Office, 1976), p. 39.

37. Jordan, "The Close and Stinking Jail," p. 141.

38. Jordan, "The Close and Stinking Jail," p. 141.

39. Ibid., p. 146.

40. American Bar Association, Commission on Correctional Facilities and Services, Statewide Jail Standards and Inspections Systems Project, *Survey and Handbook on State Standards and Inspection Legislation* (Washington, D.C.: American Bar Association, 1975), pp. 2-3.

41. Standards and Goals Commission, p. 295.

42. Ibid., pp. 294-295.

43. American Bar Association Commission on Correctional Facilities and Services, Statewide Jail Standards and Inspection Systems Project, *Statewide Jail Standards Legislation: Developmental Profiles in Four States* (Washington, D.C.: American Bar Association, 1975), pp. 2-3.

44. Hans Mattick, 'The Contemporary Jails of the United States," *Handbook of Criminology*, Daniel Glaser, ed. (Chicago: Rand-McNally, 1974), p. 781.

45. Ruggles-Brise, "American Penal System," p. 366.

46. Washington State Department of Social and Health Services, Office of Adult Corrections, *Jail Inspection Report (1972) to the 43rd Legislature* (Olympia, Wash., 1972), p. 43.

47. For example, see Robinson, *Penology*, p. 46; National Commission, p. 275; President's Commission, p. 80; Byers, op. cit., p. 220. These writers never examine assumptions necessary for this conclusion but immediately cite the effects of underfinancing.

48. Robinson, *Penology*, p. 46.

49. Standards and Goals Commission, p. 290.

50. Gail S. Funke, (written as Gail S.F. Monkman), *Cost Analysis of Community Correctional Centers* (Washington, D.C.: Correctional Economics Center, 1975) in which the average daily detention costs in a new multipurpose facility serving nine Indiana counties are estimated to be twice the current costs in separate facilities.

51. Standards and Goals Commission, p. 282.

52. U.S. Department of Justice, Law Enforcement Assistance Administration, *Nation's Jails*, p. 1.

53. National Commission, p. 275.

54. Michael Block, *Cost, Scale Economies, and Other Economic Concepts* (Washington, D.C.: Correctional Economics Center, 1976), p. 31.

55. John Mikesell, "Local Jail Operating Cost and Economic Analysis: Scale Economies in Local Jail Operation," paper presented at the Southern Economic Association, Atlanta, Georgia, 15 November 1974 (mimeo).

2 Standards: Ideas and Action

Despite reformers' good intentions through the years, today's standards are frequently a combination of desirable principles ("offender should maintain all rights of an ordinary citizen except those expressly or by implication taken from him by law"[1]), general philosophy ("Each institution should . . . develop . . . counseling programs . . . to provide to the motivation of behavioral change and interpersonal growth."[2]), and procedures ("Disciplinary hearings should be held as quickly as possible, generally not more than 72 hours after charges are made."[3]). This lack of a systematic relationship provides little clear direction for converting standards to operational realities. The examples are not atypical and are notable for their lack of specificity, criteria for compliance, and cost implications. A basic need exists for standards categorization (or better, an initial promulgation) that is relevant to both cost analysis and program decisions.

At the very least, one must look behind "black letter" standards to the supporting commentary that will assist in establishing the necessary comparability and clarity. This process will also enable an agency to relate standards to its individual goals; for example, a "community-based" emphasis may necessitate associating certain pretrial standards with corrections rather than with the courts. A priori categorization permits recognition and organization of all relevant standards.

The Correctional Economics Center, in its work with the National Advisory Commission (NAC) standards and with jail standards, developed two methods for categorizing standards. The center, under a Law Enforcement Assistance Administration grant, analyzed the cost implications of the National Advisory Commission report *Corrections*. For the state of Washington, the center analyzed the cost impact of 248 recommended minimum standards. These analytic methods were derived after exploring and rejecting other organizational schema. For example, attempting to organize standards according to "themes" of the NAC Standards ("minimize penetration"; use "least drastic means"), results in a structure too ambiguous for agency action. The Standards and Goals project (NAC Standards) used a two-tiered classification system.[4] This approach grouped the standards first by the type of change (programmatic or systemic) and then by stages of the criminal justice process (pretrial, institutions, probation, parole, and other community programs).

Categorization by Types of Change

Changes of a programmatic nature affect the activities within one stage of the criminal justice system—pretrial, probation, and so on. Examples of programmatic change advocated by the NAC Standards include:

1. Development of a full range of alternative activities within a program area (for example, educational, vocational, and counseling services in institutional-based programs)
2. Flexibility in assigning persons within any one program to the various available activities
3. Improved services for persons served by or working in the program (for example, manpower training for prison guards)

Recommendations may be program-specific or apply to more than one program simultaneously. For example, improvement in staff recruitment applies to every stage of the criminal justice system. Offenders' rights to court services apply to community as well as institutional-based programs.

Systemic change may take two forms. The first involves the program effect of altering the flow of persons through the criminal justice system. To the extent that standards implementation changes the pattern by which individuals move through the criminal justice system (for instance, pretrial diversion) or the rate of flow (for example, speedy trial, shorter sentences), certain downstream effects may occur. Implementation of standards on pretrial diversion affects the number of candidates for community corrections and for jail detention. Indeed, the criminal justice standards and goals of the state of Kansas take explicit account of this possibility. Building new facilities is contingent upon exhausting all alternatives to incarceration, including those newly recommended by the standards.[5] Greater utilization of community corrections may alter the size and composition of the prison and jail populations. Such change is more than academically relevant to the development of cost-effective planning and the channeling of savings from underutilized areas into busier programs.

The second kind of systemic change is not uniquely concerned with a single program area but affects two or more program areas simultaneously. Research, planning, and use of presentence reports are NAC-recommended activities that have implications for several stages of the system. Finally, some standards incorporate both systemic and programmatic change. A standard recommending alternatives to pretrial detention affects the pretrial program area and also implies a change in the number of persons entering the criminal justice system.

Categorization by Stages of the Criminal Justice System

This second categorization involves grouping the standards according to stages of the criminal justice system. These stages include:

1. Pretrial programs—standards relating to arrest, diversion, alternatives to detention, detention (rights of detainees to legal process, education, counseling), and speedy trial
2. Institution-based programs—improvement of facilities and services, use of work and education furloughs, staff improvements, and coordination of intake services
3. Probation—manpower development, written policies, misdemeanant probation, and statewide organization of probation
4. Parole—independent parole boards, staffing improvements, and increases in levels of services provided
5. Other community-based programs—include the establishment and greater use of halfway houses, restitution, fines, volunteer involvement, and manpower redistribution

Within any of these programmatic areas—or across them—standards may be grouped by function. This process involves subcategorizing a set of standards dealing with one program area and facilitates setting priorities by focusing on a complete set of activities.

Another categorization is by the type of cost associated by standards implementation (personnel, capital, and so on). This breakdown was used in conjunction with functional categorizations in assessing the programmatic and cost impact of state jail standards for Part II of this book, but it also may be used in isolation. The Kansas standards and goals combined several impact areas. Each overall goal (for example, improving community services to youth) was accompanied by more specific objectives or observable events (for example, by 1977, to establish community-based youth services bureaus throughout the state). These objectives, in turn, break down into basic provisions and activities, possible strategies, and implementation criteria. A matrix lists each standard, its implementation deadline, statute information, the level of government affected, its responsible agencies, and the type of action (administrative, legislative, research, appropriations) warranted to implement the standard.[6] Of course, agencies are free to select categorizations that meet their needs; the salient point is rather that some systematic grouping is necessary to reduce recommendations to manageable dimensions.

Compliance and Implementation

Before implementation can proceed, an assessment of an agency's or jurisdiction's performance relative to the standards is necessary. Such an assessment is useful not only in setting priorities for implementation, but also for identifying short- and long-term needs. First, a definition of what constitutes compliance with standards assists in establishing areas of need. In the study referenced in Part II, a jail inspection team rated jails "adequate" or "deficient" on 248 standards loosely grouped into thirty-eight categories. Although inspectors generally identified the specific problem associated with a vague standard, problems are evident:

The strip search of each prisoner shall include a thorough visual check for birthmarks, cuts, wounds, sores, bruises, scars and injuries, 'health tags' and body vermin. All physical markings and 'health tag' identifications shall be recorded and made immediately available to the appropriate jail employees and the medical professionals responsible for care of the prisoner. If feasible and particularly when force has been used during arrest all visible injuries shall be photographed.[7]

Or

Staff shall be constantly alert to prisoner depression, dissension, family rejection, loneliness, resistance to staff or programs and the effects of use of substances prohibited by facility rules or law.[8]

Even after standards have been grouped, this problem may arise. The Kansas standards referenced earlier are an example of how to preclude it. Each goal and subsequent breakdown into objectives and activities affords great clarity on what constitutes compliance. Agencies beginning this process may do well to "translate" their standards into observable events. The second standard quoted above, for example, might include subparts suggesting inmate-staff ratios, surveillance and monitoring criteria, and so on. Techniques such as this one permit ready assessment of current performance and what is required (if anything) to improve performance.

Adapting to standards may involve substantial cost or little or no cost. We discuss specific types of costs below, but we will consider the impact of this dichotomization more generally here within the context of compliance. Low-cost standards are those involving essentially procedural changes (which are no less important, although "free"). High-cost standards imply major expenditures for capital or day-to-day operations. Depending on cost and compliance, a way of establishing implementation priorities presents itself.

Low-Cost Standards

High Compliance. No need exists for immediate action; however, there may well be long-run needs for program information and technical assistance to keep the jurisdictions or agencies abreast of changes in the field in order to maintain this high compliance.

Low Compliance. Immediate action is implied for technical assistance, advisors, relevant materials, with a long-run follow-up (once compliance is achieved) similar to the case above.

High-Cost Standards

High Compliance. Again, although no immediate action is necessary, jurisdictions and agencies need to be aware of changes in the field, whether in expectations or technology. This is true regardless of the "price" of the standard, because values or priorities are not being assigned here. From a pure cost perspective, there is obvious merit in maintaining quality. Jurisdictions also need to be aware of changing situations, such as arrests, incarceration rates, and population mix.

Low Compliance. Immediate action would seem to be warranted because, by definition, the services provided are substandard. Some rating of the "most important" may have to be derived, depending on the magnitude of noncompliance and available funds. Additionally, jurisdictions may wish to examine the various combinations of resources by which to achieve compliance; in the case of institutions, for example, increasing staff or installing monitoring devices may correct inadequate surveillance. Decisions may also have to be made on strict standards adherence. A large jail in Washington would have "saved" $800,000 in remodeling costs by allowing fifty-six square feet per inmate dormitory space, rather than the sixty recommended by the standards.

Such is the range of compliance, with some appropriate action suggested. Because many programs and facilities display a combination of these phenomena, the decision maker must prioritize within the explicit contexts of compliance, cost, time, and actions required.

Costing Standards

Frequently missing from standards is an analysis of their cost impact. Funds are limited, so before an agency, jurisdiction, or state can take action, it is appropriate to know the costs any action will occasion. The level of detail described here may be superfluous for a legislature interested only in direct operating and capital costs for a program or facility. It may be very appropriate, however, when standards are to be applied systemwide or when planning requires cost projections for policy decisions.

Types of Costs

Costs can be categorized by:

1. Object of expenditure—supplies, contracts, and so on
2. Activity—pretrial detention, trial, apprehension

3. Cost center within an activity—police investigation, crime lab
4. Direct and indirect—detectives and crime information systems
5. Internal and external—police department and psychiatric services
6. Public and private—criminal justice agencies and witness expenses
7. Capital and labor—physical plant and contracted personal services

These categories are not mutually exclusive (that is, there may be an indirect capital cost borne by a private organization), but the relative emphasis in any particular instance will depend on the objectives of the analysis. The study of NAC Standards relating to corrections, for example, emphasized direct, criminal justice system expenditures because one objective was to provide criminal justice officials with implementation costs. The analysis reported in Part II, on the other hand, was principally interested in capital and noncapital resource needs.

Capital Costs. In fact, the failure to distinguish capital in public sector accounting is probably the major source of error in deriving accurate cost estimates. Assigning a dollar value to capital use is a difficult (but absolutely essential) task, because most financial information systems confound some subtle but important distinctions:

1. Some capital costs are not assigned to any government agency. There is an opportunity cost associated with public use of land, for example. One correctional institution was found to have 190 acres of fallow land zoned "rural residential" and valued at approximately $950,000. Not only could the jurisdiction realize a windfall of almost $1 million by selling, but could also benefit from future tax revenues if the land were privately held.[9]
2. External costs, such as interest on bonds, are reported as government but not an agency cost. A $10 million facility financed with thirty-year, 8 percent bonds will accrue another $17 million in interest charges alone. So, the annual capital cost is nearer $1 million annually, not the $330,000 implied on first examination.
3. Even the capital costs that are reported by an agency may confuse net additions to capital stock (for example, a new building) and maintenance of existing stock. And, in the latter case, maintenance contracts are classified in one budget category, repair parts in another, and maintenance personnel in still a third.
4. Even if different capital or capital-related costs can be identified, new equipment, structures, or land should not be charged to a single year's operating expenditures, but depreciated over the the expected useful life of the item. Excluding additions to stock or an imputed annual charge for capital use will understate an agency's operating costs; including them as a lump-sum, one-time expenditures will inflate costs in the year being

analyzed. These effects become particularly important when comparing year-to-year changes or agencies in a given time period.

One related issue requires a special note on dealing with start-up costs of new programs. The concept of capital is not limited to simply buildings, machines and acreage, but it is broad enough to include "human" capital as well. Consequently, training to give a new program's staff knowledge or specific skills that they will use over some future period of years, is properly a "capital" cost in this definition. Although it is nearly impossible (and probably not necessary) to depreciate this investment, it is important to isolate it in new programs from annual operating costs, particularly when comparisons are being made.

Joint Products and Hidden Costs. Decisions on the gross budget categories— capital/noncapital, public/private, direct/indirect, internal/external, cost center, and activity—most appropriate for a particular study are necessary in order to make a detailed cost analysis at the subagency level. The task then becomes one of adding and subtracting to derive all relevant costs, recategorizing them in a form consistent with these decisions, and resolving questions of cost allocation between agency subfunctions.

The House of Corrections Study revealed annual operating expenditures 28 percent greater than reported because many costs incurred externally were not formally included in the organization's approved budget or accounting reports. Excluding the kinds of costs described below is not unique to this jurisdiction and, in fact, is a result of local accounting practices rather than any intent to deceive.

Organizations frequently do not pay for services provided by other government agencies, such as payroll and accounting, staff recruitment and training, central purchasing, and other support services. Yet, these are real costs associated with doing business and some means should be found to distribute them. Ideally, work-load analysis of the relevant support agencies would be used to determine the proportion of their cost allocatable to the study organization(s). Alternatively, the House of Corrections overhead was estimated to be directly proportional to its share (8 percent) of the total county budget.

Grants, revenue-sharing monies, donations, and other nonappropriated funds are another external cost usually not included in routine accounting and budgeting reports. Over 10 percent of the House of Corrections' budget derived from grant funds. (Because grant periods and fund flows are seldom coextensive with budgeting cycles, selecting the time period to be covered by the analysis is especially critical when adding external and appropriated funds.) Actual operating costs are sometimes understated by excluding the value of donated goods or services and bartered items. In this case, it is necessary to impute a value by assigning a market price.

Estimates of total costs should include costs incurred by other government organizations in providing services to the criminal justice system or its clients. For example, although employment diversion at the pretrial stage typically costs the criminal justice system between \$1034 and \$1403 per "successfully" terminated client, vocational training for these persons costs from \$2000 to \$2400 per participant in 1974 dollars.[10] Alcohol treatment costs range from over \$171 per day for inpatient care at a general hospital to slightly under \$16 daily as an outpatient from a neighborhood alcoholism center.[11] Other criminal justice activities may incur similar external costs: probation departments use community mental health centers; juvenile courts refer persons to schools.

Cost Allocation

Once total agency costs have been estimated and assigned to appropriate budget categories, analyzing agency subfunctions will require a second set of cost allocation decisions. Again, the level of detail and accuracy required depend on the purpose of the study. A mayor's budget office may be interested in broad policy issues such as the dollar value of services rendered to criminal justice clients by the health department. A local sheriff on the other hand may want to know the resources devoted to pretrial as opposed to postsentence functions. Allocations in the latter case may be made in terms of certain agency goals (for example, providing services to the courts, assuring appearance at trial, rehabilitating sentenced offenders), organizational activities (for example, custody and care), or subfunctions necessary to carry out these activities (for example, booking, perimeter security, quarters supervision, feeding, sanitation, and so on).

Cost allocation estimates are theoretically complicated (but technically solvable) because two phenomena occur simultaneously. The first is called "joint products," which simply means that the process of producing one thing also produces another. Lamb chops and wool, wheat and straw, steel and smoke are common examples. More germane, incarceration results (presumably) in both improved public safety in the short run, specific deterrence in the long run and (sometimes) such "products" as higher education levels. "Factor indivisibility" refers to the fact that certain resources cannot be added in small increments. For example, one either hires a full-time court administrator or does without. A prison facility represents a large fixed cost (once the decision to build has been made) and portions of it cannot be run efficiently. On a more practical level, a sheriff may serve both as chief law enforcement officer and chief jailer; his night clerk may dispatch deputies and supervise prisoners; the chief judge may oversee court management and the probation department. In the analysis of organizational subunits, the problem becomes one of how to divide costs. Actual work-load studies or proportional allocations (based on the relative number of employees, prisoners, square footage, or some other unit) are commonly used. The House of Corrections, in the study cited above, also included a jail holding pretrial detainees; therefore, it was necessary to estimate the proportion of costs assignable only to the house for personnel performing joint functions (for example, chief security officer, hospital administrator, or training officer). Utilities charges in a county building that houses courts, jails, tax assessors, and so on can be distributed in proportion to the square footage used by each function.

Besides joint products and factor indivisibilities, other allocation problems arise from the categorization of financial data by objects of expenditure rather than cost centers or functions. The new dishwasher appears as an equipment purchase, not a food service cost. An officer funded by the police department may serve as the mayor's chauffeur. Seventeen jail staff at $121,000 annually worked in the House of Corrections. Identifying and assigning these costs requires an intimate familiarity with how the agency operates in fact, not as reported in budget documents and staffing charts.

Selecting the unit of analysis, defining cost categories, identifying data sources, and allocating costs are all intended as intermediate steps toward the real goal of total cost estimates for the agency, program, or function that will improve decision making and standards implementation.

Straightforward cost analysis certainly does not have the analytical force or decision-making significance of comparative analysis, cost effectiveness, or cost benefit. Nevertheless, it is nontrivial because it requires a consequential resource expenditure, it is a necessary precursor to these more sophisticated techniques, and (properly done) it improves the quality of information available for decision making.

Theoretically, at least, using total cost estimates (rather than partial ones) should improve the quality of decisions. Although the proof is too complicated for presentation here, it is generally the case that understating the production costs of any enterprise will result in a suboptimal resource allocation, that is, inefficiency. If capital charges are excluded from prisons' operating expenses, the cost of "producing" whatever it is they are supposed to will result in a higher incarceration rate per conviction that would otherwise have been the case. The real-world evidence for the way in which more complete information will affect public choice is visible in states and localities where citizens successfully have used the argument of high costs (among many others) in opposition to new construction. Communities may still choose to build, but with full cognizance of what they must pay. (It would be interesting, for example, to include the costs of alternative dispositions in presentence reports.)

Even if the quality of decisions does not improve, however, it is possible at least to add cost data to such unmeasurable abstractions as "public safety," "domestic tranquility," and "justice," assuming there is some reasonable assessment of and agreement on what contributes to these states of mind. Identifying the resources associated with these conditions simply supplements the ethical, legal, political, and other (sometimes more subjective) decision criteria. Only the most parochial economist would argue that cost information should receive more credence than these equally important values. But before one could even begin to answer "what price, justice?"[12] —whether it is "too much" or "too little" is a matter for collective choice—one must know what it is before making comparisons with other social priorities.

Cost Definitions

Beginning with a comprehensive, internally consistent set of cost definitions can minimize many of the above difficulties and pitfalls of cost analysis. Allocation discussions will still be required, but a clear understanding of a cost typology facilitates them. Although, in part, arbitrary, any cost typology should be workable within the accounting and budgeting formats at hand and relevant to the objectives of the study. The definitions used in the House of Corrections Study, for example, were not identical with those used in Part II or in the Standards and Goals Project. The initial distinctions in the first study were noncapital and capital, and the latter was further subdivided into "operating" (repair parts) and "new" capital (sewer main). In Washington, only new capital was of interest, but noncapital costs were broken out into staff, operating supplies, office supplies, and contractural services. Standards and Goals made its first distinction between criminal justice system costs and those external to the system, then between public or government expenditures and private ones, and, finally, between direct and indirect or overhead.[13] In each case, the study objectives, data sources, and types of information were different, and the analytical typology was designed accordingly. For example, an important cost of employment diversion is vocational training so external costs become crucial;[14] foregone contribution to national output (productivity) is a result of incarceration and opportunity cost is introduced;[15] leisure services to halfway-house residents may be privately or publicly borne.[16]

Summary

Standards have historically been viewed as a vehicle for effecting reform. The process from theoretical formulation to implementation, however, is not straightforward. Clear statement of goals, objectives and strategies, knowledge of systemic effects, definitions of compliance, and an understanding of the costs attendant to decision making are necessary precursors to the movement from ideas to operational realities.

The analysis by the Correctional Economics Center of compliance costs for recommended minimum jail standards in Washington State was no exception: variegated standards had to be prioritized, consistent cost definitions chosen, and methodologies derived to permit the translation from standards' evaluations to cost analysis. We describe this process in Part II. Chapter 3 outlines the Washington State experience (including a brief background for the study), discusses the analytic framework created to suit the purpose and characteristics of the desired results, and indicates some preliminary data analysis necessary for Chapter 4, which estimates the standards' compliance costs.

Notes

1. Standards and Goals Commission, p. 19.
2. Ibid., Standard 11.9, p. 385.
3. Ibid., Standard 2.12, p. 52.
4. The categorization process is outlined in greater detail in Correctional Economics Center, *Plan for a Cost Analysis of the Corrections Report* (Washington, D.C.: Correctional Economics Center, 1975).
5. Kansas Governor's Committee on Criminal Justice Administration and the Midwest Research Institute, *Standards and Goals for the Kansas Criminal Justice System* (1975), pp. 28-29.
6. Ibid., pp. 66-67.
7. Washington State City and County Jail Commission, *Report to the Washington State Legislature (1974)*, p. 62 (hereafter *Washington Report*). The proposed Washington Jail Standards are presented in Appendix A and are jointly referenced in parentheses. For this standard, see Appendix A, Standard 151.
·8. Ibid., p. 56 (Appendix A, Standard 132).
9. Gail S. Funke (written as Gail S.F. Monkman) and Billy L. Wayson, *Comparative Costs of State and Local Facilities* (Washington, D.C.: Correctional Economics Center, 1975) (hereafter House of Corrections).
10. Ann M. Watkins, *Cost Analysis of Correctional Standards: Pretrial Diversion* (Washington, D.C.: Correctional Economics Center, 1975), p. 50 (hereafter *Cost Analysis*).
11. Ibid., p. 53.
12. General reference is made to U.S. Department of Justice, Law Enforcement Assistance Administration, *Expenditure and Employment Data for the Criminal Justice System, 1974* (Washington, D.C.: Government Printing Office, 1976).
13. Watkins, *Cost Analysis*, pp. 6-10.
14. Ibid., p. 51.
15. Neil M. Singer and Virginia B. Wright, *Cost Analysis of Correctional Standards: Institutional-based Programs and Parole* (Washington, D.C.: Correctional Economics Center, 1976), pp. 50-57.

16. Donald Thalheimer, *Cost Analysis of Correctional Standards: Halfway Houses* (Washington, D.C.: Correctional Economics Center, 1975), p. 89.

Part II

3

The Washington State Experience

Background of the Study

To the extent one can generalize about fifty disparate entities, the state of Washington is in many ways a "typical" state. Most Washington counties are preponderantly rural, but the majority of the state's population lives in large urban areas; residents earn their living in agriculture, industry, service occupations, and government; state and local governments serve the interests of diverse constituencies, each of which has a multiplicity of objectives. Washington was, however, one of the first states to recognize the need for some form of jail inspection without enforcement powers, but for a decade, lack of resources and higher priorities made comprehensive inspection impossible. In 1972 a full-time inspector was hired. Growing public concern with jails in the early seventies led to the formation of a gubernatorial task force to study the problem, develop standards, and prepare legislation for implementation and inspection. Resultant legislation established the City and County Jail Commission to formulate minimum standards, determine the fiscal impact of implementation, and propose methods of financing improvements. As a result of legislative action in early 1975, the commission approached the Correctional Economics Center to discuss the feasibility of a joint undertaking to estimate the cost implications of standards developed in the prior year.

The Correctional Economics Center's role, generally, was to estimate the additional operating and capital costs of statewide implementation of jail standards recommended by the Washington State Jail Commission and to suggest guidelines for state and local sharing of these costs. More specifically, the objectives set forth contractually with the State Department of Social and Health Services were:

1. To estimate current operating costs for fifteen jails holding sentenced prisoners over thirty days
2. To determine resources required to bring these jails into compliance
3. To determine past and present jail population characteristics and estimate future trends
4. To suggest guidelines for determining the relative shares of upgrading costs to be borne by state and local governments[1]

A thorough description of forty-five Washington State jails and estimation of their standards compliance costs required much diverse data. Between 15

35

September and 26 November 1975, almost 18,000 data elements (395 per jail) were collected on budgets and related items, standards compliance, construction costs, jail populations, and recent changes in local criminal justice practices. Published sources provided revenue, expenditure, property valuations, and similar information for all counties for usage in deriving recommended cost-sharing guidelines.

The joint Jail Commission-CEC effort was directed at forty-five county and city jails that hold prisoners sentenced to thirty days or more. The jurisdictions that control these jails range in population from over 1 million to less than 2800; the jails themselves have average daily populations ranging from 622 to 2; jail conditions, as indicated by the commission's inspections, run the gamut from very good to poor; finally, there is great geographical disparity, from the Olympic Peninsula across the mountains to the eastern side of the state. This diversity and the first objective specified in the contract suggested usage of sampling to facilitate analysis.

Analytical Framework and Definitions

One of the first tasks in any project is establishing a structure or a framework within which analytical work can proceed. The initial need in Washington was to develop a system of arraying or categorizing jails in a fashion that would implicitly take account of, yet not be dominated by, the differences among institutions and the jurisdictions they serve. Sample selection logically follows this categorization process and serves to allow more in-depth analysis of a smaller set of jails than forty-five. Additionally, the Jail Commission suggested determining standards-implementation costs for fifteen "representative" jails that could then be extrapolated to the total population.

Because the principal focus of the study was to estimate the additional costs of meeting recommended standards, the next step in structuring the analysis should have been categorization of jails by levels of compliance with those standards that presumably would increase costs. This categorization was not possible, however, because the Jail Commission was conducting evaluations simultaneously. Time and budget constraints in any study invariably create a tradeoff between the quantity of data that can be collected and the amount that can be analyzed. Increasing the quantity of data to improve projections means sacrificing detail. Given this dilemma, the important criterion for choosing becomes how the results will be used and who will use them. A legislative committee, for example, is probably more interested in the accuracy of overall projections, the local sheriff in the cost of upgrading a specific jail. The policy question at the state level must address all jails in the state in terms of their conditions, quality of service, comparisons among their operations, and so on. The county commission, on the other hand, is primarily concerned with how their facility is operating and only secondarily with how well it compares to other jurisdictions.

Sampling became a necessary expedient for two reasons: the short time frame of the study dictated simultaneous Jail Commission inspections and CEC analysis; by grouping jurisdictions for sample selection, we avoided performing repeated in-depth studies for jurisdictions exhibiting similar, cost-related characteristics. Jurisdictional population was selected as the basis for sample generation for the following reasons:

1. Jurisdictional population data was readily available, common to localities, and completely objective.
2. Jail populations and capacities were closely related to jurisdictional size.
3. Jurisdictions in all geographical regions were represented in the population categories.
4. Jails at all levels of standards compliance were represented in each population category.
5. Extrapolations were possible within population categories, because scale of operation affected upgrading costs.

The forty-five jails were distributed among four population types stratified by jurisdictional size, and a proportionate sample was randomly selected from each type as representative of the eleven city and thirty-four county facilities. Table 3-1 shows the total population sorted by jurisdictional size and the results of sample selection (in parentheses). It had already been decided that the analysis would go beyond merely looking at a sample and include as much input from as many jails as possible; through the analysis, the sample was viewed as a minimum data base. Consequently, current operating-cost data were compiled on forty-five jails, capital-upgrading costs were estimated for all facilities, and operating costs at compliance were computed for bases of fifteen and twenty-three jails, which, when extrapolated to forty-five, resulted in more reliable cost estimates.

Table 3-1
Stratification of Jail Population and Sample

Type	Jurisdiction Size[a]	County	City	Total
1	500,000+	1 (1)		1 (1)
2	100,000-500,000	6 (2)	1 (1)	7 (3)
3	20,000-100,000	16 (5)	3 (1)	19 (6)
4	Under 20,000	11 (3)	7 (2)	18 (5)
Total		34 (11)	11 (4)	45 (15)

[a]1974 census data, Division of Municipal Corporations, Office of the State Auditor.

Standards Analysis and Categorization

The 248 standards that the Jail Commission[2] developed and used as a basis for jail inspections and evaluations were designed to be as inclusive as possible. Jails were rated "adequate" or "deficient" on items such as sufficient living space, admissions procedures, visitation, inmate privileges, fire suppression equipment, and staff training. As formulated, the standards were inclusive, not prioritized, and implied different magnitudes and types of expenditures to reach compliance.

A mix of objective and subjective evaluations also characterized the standards. A jail's compliance with some standards was readily visible ("Detention and Correction facilities shall provide indoor program and recreation areas"),[3] but other standards required interviewing jail staff and assuming the staff's perceptions were accurate ("Staff shall be constantly alert to prisoner depression, dissension, family rejection, loneliness").[4]

From an analytic perspective, the introduction of ordering or structure is necessary not only to organize findings, but also to aid in the establishment of priorities. General program priorities are the responsibility of the Jail Commission, the legislature, and local communities. What was done in this study, however, was to array the results in such a way that the compliance and cost variables were explicit. This arrangement permits the establishment of priorities based on costs, time, and type of effort (for example, legislation, appropriations, and technical assistance) required to bring all jails into compliance.

The standards were "ordered" in several ways to facilitate analysis. The first involved collapsing the Jail Commission's thirty-eight general classes into eighteen related functions:

Plant	Transportation
Electrical	Security and Control
Water	Discipline
Heating and Ventilation	Health Care
Administration and Staffing	Food
Records	Personal Care Items
Admission	Sanitation and Safety
Classification	Inmate Services
Release	Communications

Within these cost centers, the standards were examined across the dimension of cost: whether compliance involved costs, the areas in which these costs would occur (personnel, supplies, services, equipment, and plant) and the estimated magnitude of the cost (high, medium, or low).

This information on costs and a tabulation of standards compliance by each jail made it possible to identify various combinations of compliance status and cost implication, in effect to construct a matrix for each jail across cost and compliance dimensions. There exist numerous combinations of compliance and cost impact. For example, a jail might be complying with 95 percent of the standards, yet the 5 percent deficiency could have substantial cost implications. Moreover, these cost implications might be for immediate operating problems (quality of food, for example) or for longer-term capital improvements, such as added recreation space. Conversely, a jail operating at 60 percent of compliance might be deficient in essentially costless, procedural areas (preparing an organization chart). Or a jail at 60 percent compliance might display both costless and cost noncompliance.

Subsequent discussion and analysis of data generated from Washington State jails will outline standards-compliance rates, which provide a convenient method for summarizing the results of the Jail Commission evaluations. Before discussing specific data, however, various concepts related to cost are necessary to complete the analytical framework.

Definition of Current Operating Costs

We discussed the need for consistent and appropriate cost definitions for implementing cost analysis in Chapter 2. The definitions used for Washington State were determined by the study objectives and the budgeting and accounting system used statewide by local governments. Current operating costs in Washington are distinguished by their relation to capital cost elements; these costs are defined as all costs that are necessary for maintenance and operation of a jail over a specific time period. They include both noncapital operating costs (personnel, supplies, and services) and capital operating costs (capital outlays, some capital improvements, and machinery and equipment). Current, noncapital operating costs are the daily costs associated with caring for an inmate population. Such costs include admission, release, administrative duties and record keeping, medical care, custodial services, feeding, heating, and so on. Capital costs are one-time acquisitions associated with plant and equipment (buildings, fences, roadways, and major equipment) and are not included in daily operating costs, although a true annual cost figure for "usage" (depreciation) would ideally be included as part of operating costs.

Current operating costs per inmate day (average daily cost, or ADC) are calculated by dividing the total operating budget of a particular jail by the average daily population of that facility. By comparison, operating costs at capacity are derived by using the same total operating budget for a facility, but the total number of bed days available (jail capacity multiplied by 365) is the significant cost determinant. The operating costs at capacity represent the cost of operation if each bed in the jail were always occupied and are usually substantially lower for jails in Washington State, because many operate below capacity.

To be as informative as possible, budget data should be structured around specific functions within a cost center, which, in turn, is related to an organization's objectives. However, Washington State and local budget data are maintained by object of expenditure rather than by function (Appendix A describes this accounting system). In terms of upgrading to standards, cost centers are more useful than object-of-expenditure accounting in identifying the area in which a jail is deficient. For example, if a jail is deficient in its surveillance and security areas, one upgrading cost may involve more personnel; or conversely, and perhaps more usefully, if a jail is understaffed the functional areas in which this understaffing occurs can be identified. For the decision maker, cost centers mean greater information on where new dollars should be directed and on the results that should be expected. Upgrading estimates will be displayed by expenditures categories, which include explanations regarding cost center effects and implications.

Data availability problems necessitated delimiting operating costs to data that were available for all jails. However, although total operating cost information is less than complete for certain budgetary items, it is comparable across all jails and includes similar personnel, supplies, services and capital outlays (where applicable). The trade-off required to assure data consistency was that certain limitations are inherent in operating-cost data.

Excluded Costs. Time limitations did not permit an estimation of certain nonbudgeted items, which, nevertheless, should be included in a total cost analysis for any jail.

One problem occurred because the accounting system used throughout Washington State local governments does not lend itself readily to total cost accounting, which assigns resource use regardless of its source. Actual and appropriated budgetary amounts indicated in the county auditor's or city comptroller's report are specific only to the General Fund of the jurisdiction. Other funding sources, such as federal, state, or local grants, and revenue-sharing monies, were not always included, even though the services purchased with these monies are necessary for jail operations. Frequently, however, funds from other sources were for salaries, and the majority of these were known. Costs from other funding sources were included whenever possible.

External Costs. Some jails received services from other agencies and it was extremely difficult to extricate their cost from other sources (for example, deriving the costs of medical services to inmates from the county health officer). This kind of data problem emerged most frequently for costs external to the jail operation. For example, due to the billing procedures for utilities and the location of many jails in buildings serving a variety of other functions, these costs simply could not be estimated within the time constraints of this study.

Joint Budgets. The main data sources were county auditor's reports and budgets, and city comptroller's reports and budgets. Many of the smaller jurisdictions combined or completely included the jail budgets in the sheriff's or police budget. Occasionally it was possible to identify all relevant expenditures, but more frequently sheriff and police budgets were indicated in a way that prevented totally accurate estimation of jail expenditures.

Other Limitations. Further data collection problems resulted from ways in which auditors' and comptrollers' reports presented information. Small jurisdictions often did not use standard accounting procedures; contracted services (included in "professional services") were not always identifiable within the budgets. To correct for these problems, telephone interviews were conducted with twenty-eight jails to supplement existing data, and resolve data discrepancies. These interviews were sometimes the only source of budgetary information. Jail Commission staff assisted by gathering all published reports on costs during on-site visits.

Cost Impact of Standards

The final tool developed to facilitate cost analysis synthesizes cost-center categorization of standards with cost data found in the Washington State object-of-expenditure accounting system. It is displayed as Appendix C. The Washington State accounting system, called BARS (budgeting, accounting and reporting system) consists of four major expenditure categories with several subcategories. (See Appendix B for a more detailed description of the BARS system.) Significant for this study are the four main BARS categories (personnel, supplies, services, and capital) and two subcategories that distinguish between office and operating supplies.

For the purposes of estimating compliance costs, it was necessary first to distinguish standards that could be implemented with relatively few resources from those requiring additional staff, supplies, or facilities. Forty-six percent (113) of the standards required no or very few new resources and were not considered in deriving upgrading costs. Of the remaining 133, 27 were related to capital improvements and 106 to noncapital items (63 implied staff costs and 43 implied other operating costs).

Because *Cost Impact of Standards* (Appendix C) serves as the transition between standards and cost analysis, a professional consensus of opinion was used to determine potential impact.[5] Standards are differentiated as either having or not having cost impact with respect to particular expenditure categories; no magnitude is implied other than possibly when standards are noted as having impact in more than one expenditure category. For standards with negligible cost impact, no impact is noted. An example is the standard titled "notice of search,"[6] which requires conspicuous posting of notices; the supplies and personnel costs necessary are virtually nonexistent. Impacting upon two or more expenditure categories, however, does not necessarily mean that a standard will have greater implementation cost. For example, the community resource[7] standard has impact in each of the four major expenditure categories. Jail staff might implement this standard by utilizing educational services available in the community by transporting prisoners to community colleges or other local public or private services. Thus, only staff time (and perhaps an equipment cost for vehicles) would be necessary for transporting prisoners. By comparison, the standard requiring staff the same sex as prisoners impacts upon only the personnel expenditure category;[8] but this standard could have very significant cost implications if a jail implements it by hiring round-the-clock female correctional officers.

Results of Data Analysis in Washington State

Compliance Rates

Compliance rates were calculated by dividing the number of standards rated "adequate" by the total number of applicable standards, expressed in percentages. Any standards not relevant to a particular facility were excluded to avoid deflating the rates. The standards categorization process made possible determination of specific compliance rates by function (for example, compliance with respect to physical plant or health care) or along cost dimensions (capital costs, personnel costs, or no cost).

Total compliance rates including forty-five facilities and 248 standards were the most general summarization of the conditions in Washington State jails. As shown in Table 3-2, the distribution of rates was skewed toward high compliance with almost 50 percent of the standards rated adequate in 90-100 percent of the cases. A two-person team of the commission's staff performed most evaluations, so it may be assumed that the distribution probably resulted from the nature of the standards themselves rather than differences in their application. It does suggest, however, that certain standards may not be sufficiently stringent to evaluate the quality of services being provided. Low-compliance standards—though few—are heavily biased toward high cost capital improvements. For example, twenty-five of the thirty-four standards rated 40 percent or less relate to plant (inmate housing, activities space, visiting, offices, and so on), electrical, heating, and water. The physical plant cost center, which contained twenty-seven standards, had an overall compliance rate of 49 percent for all jails. Determination of compliance rates specific to individual standards or cost centers was also useful because unique deficiencies of a jail (or group of jails)

Table 3-2
Distribution of All Standards by Compliance Group

Compliance Group (percent)	Standards Number	Percent
90-100	123	49.8
80-89	29	11.7
70-79	22	8.9
60-69	25	10.2
50-59	14	5.7
40-49	8	3.2
30-39	7	2.8
20-29	11	4.5
10-19	8	3.2
0-9	0	0
Total	247[a]	100.0

[a]One standard, which required reporting serious incidents and emergencies to the Jail Commission, is not applicable to any jurisdiction.

became apparent. Consequently it became more clear what was required to attain compliance with particular standards.

As might be expected, there was an overall high compliance for standards requiring minimal or no resources. Minor deficiencies came to light in many procedural areas, such as failure to inform non-English-speaking visitors of contraband penalties.[9] Compliance with standards requiring additional resources, on average, was less than with no-cost ones. For example, the subset of jails representing the smallest jurisdictions had an average compliance rate of 80 percent for all standards. For standards with cost implications, compliance ranged from 42 to 94 percent, with an average rate of 71 percent.

Personnel compliance had a wider range (29-98 percent) than total cost standards compliance rates. Generally, it tended to be lower, with thirty-three of the jails complying with less than 80 percent of the personnel cost standards. Less than 20 percent of the jails complied with standards for pre- and in-service training,[10] classification committees,[11] medical screening,[12] daily exercise,[13] and supervision of volunteers.[14]

The average capital compliance for all jails was only 49 percent—substantially lower than for any other group of standards. The range was from 4 to 98 percent. Smaller, type-3 jails were generally in worse condition (43 percent compliance) than the larger ones (type 2) serving the state's population centers, which met 72 percent of the capital standards. The commission staff's recommendations for new facilities were consistent with this overall analysis: seventeen were so poor that they required replacement; twenty-six needed major or minor remodeling.

Space for support services (kitchen, laundry, and clothing storage) was comparatively adequate, even though no more than 68 percent of the jails met any one of these standards.[15] Indoor recreation areas were almost totally absent (14 percent),[16] followed closely by lack of living quarters[17] (16 percent) that provided "reasonable" privacy, continuous surveillance, and healthful surroundings. A need for medical examining rooms, visiting space, and improved booking areas also was apparent.[18] Cell lighting, ventilation, and air conditioning standards were met, respectively, in only 44, 51, and 54 percent of the jails.[19] The distribution of compliance rates are compared in Table 3-3.

Physical plant conditions, medical services, institutional security, program availability, and a host of other factors described above formed the basis for estimating additional resources needed to achieve standards compliance in forty-five city and county jails.

Utilization Rate

Utilization rate is the ratio of a jail's average daily population to its rated capacity, expressed as a percentage. When utilization rate is high, a jurisdiction's operating costs should be proportionately lower than if the jail housed a smaller number of inmates; in this situation, average daily cost begins to approach per-bed cost.

In 1974, only two Washington jails frequently exceeded capacity. All others operated at considerably less than rated capacity; statewide the average occupancy was 57 percent of a total of 3306 beds. Table 3-4 also summarizes some descriptive statistics about relative spending, average daily populations, and total available capacity by jurisdictional size.

Table 3-3
Number of Jails

Compliance Group (percent)	Total Compliance Rate (248)	Personnel Compliance Rate (63)	Capital Compliance Rate (27)
90	4	2	3
80	18	10	5
70	19	15	5
60	3	12	1
50	1	4	7
less than 50	0	2	24

Table 3-4
Data Comparisons for Washington State Jails by Population Type[a]

Type	Budget Total	Budget Percent of State Total	Population ADP	Population Percent of State Total	Capacity Rated Capacity	Capacity Percent of State Total	Utilization Rate (percent)
1	$3,234,090	41.3	622	32.8	750	22.7	82.9
2	2,703,820	34.6	719	38.0	1316	39.8	54.6
3	1,361,378	17.4	431	22.8	848	25.7	50.8
4	516,091	6.6	121	6.4	392	11.8	30.9
Total	$7,815,379	99.9	1893	100.0	3306	100.0	

[a]Data collected and generated by the Correctional Economics Center and the Washington State City and County Jail Commission, September-November 1975. The Economics Center is responsible for all data analyses.

Base-Year Budget Data

Analysis of operating expenditures for all forty-five jails in Washington State in their present condition must precede determination of standards implementation costs. Available budgetary data may be compiled and displayed in a variety of ways, depending upon the reason for the analysis. The perspective established by the scope and objectives of the Washington State study often required viewing each jail's expenditures separately, although aggregating within jurisdictional size groupings (established during sample selection) is necessary during estimation of upgrading costs.

Because cost center data were not available, expenditure information was collected or generated for all forty-five jails and differentiated into four main accounting categories: personnel, supplies, services, and capital. This grouping permitted observation of general relationships among the types of expenditures of various-sized jails, as well as comparison of these expenditures and compliance with all 248 standards or with a particular functional cost center. All data were from 1974 sources and documents and are in 1974 dollars. For more generally informative purposes, total costs for 1974, total annual unit costs, and average daily costs (ADC) were calculated, although these were always presented disaggregated with respect to expenditure categories to prevent obscuring or "losing" data.

In 1974 a statewide jail budget of $7,815,379 was expended as follows: 76 percent of all costs were personnel costs, whereas supplies were 15 percent, services 8 percent, and capital only 1 percent. For individual jails, the personnel costs ranged from 40 to 94 percent, and supplies expenditures varied from 4 to

54 percent. Services varied 21 percent. The range for capital expenditures is not discussed because there are data inconsistencies in this area.

Average daily costs appear in Table 3-5. These are particularly important because they represent useful measures for the decision maker who is concerned with inmate flows through a jail and with their effect upon fluctuations in operating costs. The inclusion of the noncapital budget (column 4) as well as total average daily costs is intended to correct for difficulties in determining comparable capital expenditures for many jails. Average daily costs for 1974 average daily populations (ADP) ranged from $3.87 to $62.75; the statewide average daily cost was $11.31 for a total ADP of 1893. On the other hand, per-bed costs (using rated capacity rather than ADP as the divisor), which do not appear in Table 3-5, reached a maximum of $13.49 and a minimum of $1.37 for a statewide-rated total capacity of 3306. The average daily costs are determined by the magnitude of the ADPs and per-bed costs by the rated capacities of the jails, which may be determined by jurisdictional needs as much as by intended design capacity. Per-bed costs are significant because they help standardize the cost fluctuations caused by the variation in ADPs. Costs at capacity reflect each jail's potential lowest costs within existing budgets if every bed in the jail were filled; they provide another measure of comparability.

Generally, average daily costs increase as the ADP for the jail decreases (see Table 3-6). Smaller jails are more costly because a core of basic services must be available regardless of the number of inmates housed. Costs at capacity do not display the same relationship, although it is likely this pattern would emerge in a larger sample.

Table 3-5
Average Daily Costs for Forty-five Washington Jails (1974)

Jail Type No.	Total Compliance Rate (percent)	Total ADC (BARS 10-60)	ADC Excluding Capital	ADC Personnel (BARS 10)	ADC Supplies and Services (BARS 20-30)
1 1	97	$14.24	$14.08	$11.29	$2.79
2 1	93	16.67	16.47	12.23	4.24
2	88	5.51	5.51	4.11	1.40
3	84	29.93	29.21	20.33	8.88
4	81	12.00	11.85	8.59	3.26
5	79	9.37	9.37	7.53	1.84
6	78	15.83	15.83	12.58	3.25
7	65	6.72	6.64	4.69	1.95
Mean	81	$13.71	$13.55	$10.01	$3.54
Median	81				

Table 3-5 (continued)

Jail Type No.	Total Compliance Rate (percent)	Total ADC (BARS 10-60)	ADC Excluding Capital	ADC Personnel (BARS 10)	ADC Supplies and Services (BARS 20-30)
3 1	90	$14.64	$14.64	$12.09	$2.55
2	88	8.33	8.33	6.01	2.32
3	88	13.73	13.55	11.87	1.68
4	87	7.88	7.01	6.24	.77
5	86	12.99	12.70	9.90	2.80
6	86	12.84	12.84	10.64	2.20
7	85	12.46	11.37	6.54	4.83
8	80	12.96	12.70	10.90	1.80
9	79	11.55	11.55	10.12	1.43
10	79	10.56	10.56	6.84	3.72
11	78	4.57	4.57	3.79	0.78
12	78	3.04	2.81	1.65	1.16
13	76	9.42	9.42	6.13	3.29
14	75	3.87	3.87	2.43	1.44
15	75	8.82	8.80	6.49	2.31
16	74	7.27	7.26	5.89	1.37
17	74	20.07	19.89	17.68	2.21
18	72	11.01	10.91	8.95	1.96
19	53	12.58	12.25	9.73	2.52
Mean	79	$10.45	$10.26	$ 8.10	$2.16
Median	79				
4 1	90	$24.12	$23.96	$19.93	$4.03
2	87	17.71	17.71	12.47	5.24
3	88	29.23	29.23	24.36	4.87
4	87	19.15	19.15	16.54	2.61
5	84	6.87	6.87	5.19	1.68
6	83	7.32	7.32	5.28	2.04
7	85	11.18	10.94	6.86	4.08
8	83	23.58	23.58	20.98	2.60
9	79	4.99	4.99	3.14	1.85
10	77	25.80	25.80	11.93	13.87
11	73	19.61	19.61	10.96	8.65
12	74	11.07	11.07	8.61	2.46
13	75	62.75	62.39	53.52	8.87
14	70	25.53	25.53	24.02	1.51
15	70	8.30	7.39	5.06	2.33
16	69	6.87	6.65	2.27	4.38
17	60	7.33	7.44	5.80	1.64
18	89	(10.05)	7.27	4.05	3.22
Mean	79	$17.87	$17.61	$13.38	$4.23
Median	81				
Mean, all jails	80%	$14.01	$13.80	$10.58	$3.22

Table 3-6

Average Daily Costs for Sample Jails by Diminishing Average Daily Population (1974)

Jail			Average Daily Cost	
Type No.	ADP	Capacity	ADP	Capacity
1 1	622	750	$14.25	$11.81
2 1	96	196	$12.00	$5.88
2	47	150	9.37	2.93
3	35	101	16.67	5.78
Type average			$12.68	$4.86
3 1	29	66	$11.55	$5.08
2	25	48	8.82	4.59
3	22	41	12.57	5.08
4	18	58	14.64	4.54
5	12	34	3.87	1.38
6	5	22	12.46	3.28
Type average			$10.65	$4.27
4 1	6	20	$ 7.32	$2.20
2	5	7	11.07	7.91
3	4	13	14.17	5.45
4	4	21	29.23	5.57
5	3	10	19.61	5.88
Type average			$16.28	$5.40

Summary

Compliance rates and 1974 budgets are necessary baseline data for determining the additional funds needed to upgrade local Washington jails. In order to derive compliance costs, however, it was necessary to develop an analytical framework to make the 248 standards more manageable conceptually. A cost impact matrix isolated the standards relevant to this study in 18 functional areas; a second matrix constructed to show which cost standards were not compiled with by simple jails provided a "crosswalk" between specific deficiencies and the types of resources needed for improvement. Chapter 4 explains the process and results of estimating the dollar value of these additional resources.

Notes

1. "Statement of Work," *Washington State Jail Survey Project*, contract between the Correctional Economics Center and the Washington State Department of Social and Health Services, August 1975.

2. *Washington Report*, pp. 46-94.

3. Ibid., p. 50 (Appendix A, Standard 104).

4. Ibid., p. 56 (Appendix A, Standard 132).

5. Interviews with Dennis Paulson of the Washington State Jail Commission and James Murphy of the Potomac Justice Foundation, October 1975.

6. *Washington Report*, p. 94 (Appendix A, Standard 342).

7. Ibid., p. 86 (Appendix A, Standard 290).

8. Ibid., p. 56 (Appendix A, Standard 130).

9. Ibid., p. 69 (Appendix A, Standard 342).

10. Ibid., p. 57 (Appendix A, Standard 133).

11. Ibid., p. 63 (Appendix A, Standards 163 and 164).

12. Ibid., p. 77 (Appendix A, Standard 233).

13. Ibid., p. 87 (Appendix A, Standard 297).

14. Ibid., p. 85 (Appendix A, Standard 298).

15. Ibid., pp. 50-52 (Appendix A, Standards 107, 108, 114, and 115).

16. Ibid., p. 50 (Appendix A, Standard 104).

17. Ibid., (Appendix A, Standard 101).

18. Ibid., pp. 50-52 (Appendix A, Standards 109, 112, and 117).

19. Ibid., p. 53 (Appendix A, Standards 119, 124, and 125).

4 Standards Implementation Costs

The budget data and jail evaluations (compliance rates) discussed in Chapter 3 provided the foundation for assessing current costs and jail conditions. The next step was to determine the costs of raising deficient jails to compliance with the recommended minimum standards. The general approach was to use known information about the sample to estimate for the population. This was consistent with study objectives to derive total rather than individual jail costs for the legislature. In the case of capital costs, architectural firms specializing in correctional facilities furnished estimates. For noncapital, operating costs, the problem was more complicated and required use of several analytical techniques. Estimates for personnel, food, medical, and program costs were each derived in slightly different fashion, depending on the information available. Thus, more reliable and more extensive cost estimates were possible than if only a single methodological approach had been used.

Operating Standards Implementation Costs

Areas of Deficiency

Estimation of the dollar magnitude of deficiencies in the day-to-day operation of a jail involves several steps. First, only standards pertaining to such operations are selected for analysis and standards possessing few or no cost implications may be eliminated. Grouping deficiencies into functional areas permits observation of a total service unit rather than a single standard or line-item expenditure. A cost impact matrix (Appendix C) facilitates cost estimation by associating service unit deficiencies with specific standards and with the kind of cost most likely to be affected.

Operating (or noncapital) costs are those incurred in "running" a jail. They include such items as staff, food, paper, medicine, utilities. For convenience, operating costs may be classified as follows:

1. Personnel
2. Office supplies
3. Operating supplies
4. Services

This classification corresponds to the BARS categories used in Washington and provides a convenient method of determining where in a jurisdiction's budget the cost impact of standards compliance will occur. The following description of some deficient functional areas in Washington's jails identifies compliance costs along this dimension.

Administration and Staffing. The overall compliance rate for the forty-five jails surveyed was 51 percent. This cost center encompassed surveillance, a requirement that some staff be of the same sex as inmates, and training. Forty-two percent of the jails conformed to the same-sex, twenty-four-hour supervision standard, 30 percent provided continuous surveillance, and only 14 percent provided proper pre- and in-service training.

Achieving compliance with standards such as these may involve substantial cost to a jurisdiction. For example, covering one twenty-four-hour post, each day of the year requires at least 4.5 man years, or 4.5 staff members working forty-hour weeks.[1] The presence of prisoners of each sex in the jail raises minimum required staff to nine persons. The cost considerations attendant to these requirements are substantial for small jails housing only a few persons.

Training recommendations create other new personnel costs. The National Advisory Commission's report *Corrections* suggests one hundred hours of training for new staff during the first year and forty hours of in-service training each year thereafter.[2] Even if the training program itself is offered free of charge,[3] coverage for participating personnel who are absent from normal duties will be necessary. The principal impact of compliance with administration and staffing standards, therefore, will be on personnel costs.

Classification. This cost center includes classification activities such as interviews, review, and classification of inmates. Only 18 percent of the jails had the recommended classification committee. Deficiency in that standard implies deficiencies in other standards that relate to the committee's duties. The impact on staff needs may be substantial, because a corrections facility requires a three-person committee, a detention facility, a two-person committee. In many cases, current staff simply were not available to form a committee, and new staff would be required. Other classification costs were minimal.

Health Care. Jails generally seemed to be providing adequate health care. However, one standard required each jail to obtain a health history at admission (within twelve hours of booking) and an assessment of that history by a medical professional within forty-eight hours. Eighty-two percent of the jails failed to carry out these procedures. Because jail staff are seldom qualified medical professionals, implementation ordinarily would require outside contracting for such services. The upgrading cost of this standard, then, would be reflected in the services object of expenditure, which includes such contracting.

Inmate Services. This cost center includes education, training, recreation, release services, and other services to inmates. The standards call on the jails to arrange for such programs as high-school equivalency training, college courses, and trade-school programs, to fully explore and utilize local community resources, and to provide staff supervision of these activities. Again, compliance significantly affects personnel costs, as well as services, and perhaps involves some small costs for supplies and materials.

Communications. These standards generally relate to inmate communications with the outside world, including telephone usage, mail privileges, and visiting. Compliance with the first two areas was relatively high; compliance was not costly because rule changes were the major need. Visiting regulations, however, had substantial personnel-cost implications, because each prisoner, whether awaiting trial or sentenced, was to have a minimum of three hours visitation per week. Supervising and conducting visits may require staff for admitting visitors, searching, general surveillance, and special arrangements such as confidential consultation. Jails without secure booking areas (a not uncommon problem) faced additional monitoring duties associated with unrestricted entry of persons into the jail during these hours.

Other Problem Areas. Of less significance in terms of cost implications and because of high compliance were the functional areas of records, food service, personal care, and sanitation and safety. Admissions deficiencies could be remedied by providing copies of facility rules, oral orientation, and the purchase of a log book. Work-release supervision could not generally be corrected without capital (structural) improvements such as isolated living areas. Disciplinary hearings needed improved procedures; rules needed to be posted. Food-service delivery was usually good, but several jails served only two meals in a fourteen-hour period. Correcting this problem would involve additional operating-supplies costs or, in the cases where meals are catered, an increase in cost for services.

In general, then, the increase in operating costs to bring jails to compliance with the recommended minimum standards would include greater expenditures for personnel, services, some operating supplies, and minimal office supplies.

Case Study Methodology

Estimating the costs of improved human-service delivery as envisioned in the recommended minimum standards required not only structuring the standards and their cost implications, but also developing an appropriate methodology as well. Earlier discussion noted the stratification of the standards along different dimensions, such as cost impact or type of cost. Stratification is important for prioritization, even without a cost analysis, but it is critical if estimates are to be meaningful. A jail may have a low compliance rate that is occasiond by inadequacies in areas costing little or nothing to correct, and using such a "raw" compliance rate would lead to overstatement in calculating upgrading costs. Fortunately, it was possible not only to identify the cost standards but to pinpoint within that classification standards with the greatest cost implications. This factor contributed greatly to the reliability of the cost estimation that was performed.

Of the 248 recommended minimum standards, 63 have some personnel cost implications (and some supplies and services costs as well) and 43 more imply additional costs for supplies and services only. Overwhelmingly, the greatest impact was in the area of personnel costs; the jails of Washington, not atypically, spend 76 percent of their monies on wages, salaries, and fringe benefits. Another 8 percent is allocated to services such as medical care and education. Except for the few jails providing inadequate nutrition, the dollar impact on other operating costs was minimal; increments to such costs of less than $100 are ignored in the calculations.

Calculating the additional costs associated with standards compliance is a complex process and is basically inseparable from the individual jail. The ways in which resources (land, labor, capital, management) may be combined to operate a jail are as numerous as the jurisdictions themselves. Ideally, each of the forty-five jurisdictions would have been studied in depth so that "personalized" cost increments could have been calculated. Given the time and scope of the study, however, it was necessary to select a random sample and use a case study method, which may be applied by other states and localities similarly constrained by time and funds.

The evaluations performed by the Jail Services Commission provided the basis for analyzing compliance and grouping deficiencies by functional area for each jail. Extensive interviews with Commission staff were then conducted regarding the fifteen sample jails; seven more were later selected and included in this review and evaluation so that in-depth case studies were obtained for twenty-three, or 51 percent of the forty-five city and county jails. The additional jails were well distributed with regard to compliance, size, and geographical region, as was the original sample.

Each case study was essentially an analysis of a jail's deficient functional areas and the relevant cost standards within those areas. The additional personnel, supplies, and services required to achieve compliance were estimated for each jail within the context of its own operating status. These results were then used to estimate compliance costs for jails not surveyed. This approach, by providing insight into many real operating situations, avoided blanket assumptions about cost increases and permitted realistic personnel calculations for a state having many small jails.

Cumulative Effect of Standards. The prevalence of small jails (44 percent had daily populations under ten; two-thirds had twenty-five or less) highlighted a staffing/workload phenomenon peculiar to this group. In such jails, a single individual rarely performs only one job assignment. Thus a correctional officer may supervise feeding, monitor visiting, and sit on a classification committee. If a jail were deficient in one or two such areas, the current staff possibly could handle the slight additional workload. However, a cumulative effect occurs if a jail is deficient in several areas, such as supervision of inmate education programs, training, physical exercise, volunteer services, and visiting. Complying with one or two of these items would not involve additional staff. However, the cumulative effect of improvement in all areas would be sufficient to warrant hiring an additional, full-time person.[4] In this way the problem of factor indivisibility may be circumvented. The implication for a particular jurisdiction is some preservation of its individual choice and discretion, rather than, for example, fulfillment of arbitrary requirements to increase staff. The point at which more personnel are necessary, of course, varies with each jurisdiction.

Personnel Cost Estimation

All cost estimations and extrapolations were developed for jail type, because facilities with wide population differences are not operationally comparable. The very largest jail in the state had no deficiencies (and was also a sample jail), so estimates are for the remaining forty-four jails. Index numbers, adjustments, and alternative estimation procedures appear in Appendixes D and E, but are summarized here.

It was possible to estimate personnel compliance costs in three ways, given the existence of both the original sample and the extended sample (twenty-three). The resultant man-year and cost recommendations were very similar. For the first two methods, a fourteen-jail sample (partitioned by type and excluding the largest sample jail) could be used to extrapolate to the remaining thirty jails or the extended sample used and extrapolated to the thirty jails less those additionally surveyed. The last method was used here: twenty-two jails were used as the basis for estimating costs of the remaining twenty-two. For explanatory purposes, the focus here will be limited to the nineteen jails in the medium-small category (type 3).

Estimation Adjustments. Variation in jail populations, staffing levels, and compliance with standards required some adjustments before the sample could be used to estimate for the population. For example, a jail might already possess sufficient staff, perhaps poorly distributed, to remedy its deficiencies; this factor had to be controlled so that unnecessary staff (and costs) were not recommended. Also, a particular jail might have a different compliance rate than the sample and it would be important to avoid recommending more staff for a high-compliance facility. To compensate for these factors, index numbers were introduced and applied to the sample results before generalizing to the balance of the population. One index number was used to normalize differences in compliance rates; the other was used to control for potentially adequate staffing levels.

Cost projections were made for the population minus the sample. These projections were made for the jails of a particular type because it would have been analytically presumptuous to assign new personnel and costs to a specific jail without in-depth study. Thus, all cost estimates for this group are presented as totals.

Man-year Estimation. Case studies of nine of the nineteen type-3 jails revealed personnel standards compliance rates ranging from 29 percent to 82 percent and staffs of 1.5 to 10 persons out of a total of 47.5 current staff. Individual assessment of each sample jail's needs for additional personnel to perform surveillance, training, classification, and program functions resulted in recommendations for an additional 41.6 man years—almost double the current staff complement—an increase of 4.6 man years per jail. Had the remaining jails possessed precisely the same compliance and staffing characteristics as the sample, straight-line extrapolation would have mandated a total of 87.4 new man years for the nineteen jails. (We remind the reader that all extrapolations are to the total jails not surveyed in depth because individual distinctions were not possible.) However, corrections were made, with index adjustments for differences in compliance rates and potentially adequate staff. First, the ratio of the compliance rates of the sample to those of the population (less the sample) was obtained. The weight of the slightly higher population compliance rates reduced the recommended man years from 45.8 to 39.1. Comparing the average sample jail staff to the average staff size of the remaining jails yielded a similar ratio. The higher average staff in the population further reduced the personnel recommendation to 31.7 man years, for a total downward adjustment of 31 percent.

Cost Estimation. Current average annual salaries for correctional officers were used to translate the man year figures into cost estimates. Because the sample jails were treated individually, each jail's average annual salary was multiplied by its newly required man years to arrive at a cost for compliance in areas necessitating more personnel. For the remaining jails, an overall average annual salary was applied to the 31.7 new man years. During the first year of standards compliance, the additions to personnel costs for type-3 jails were estimated at $430,017 for the sample and $291,989 for the remaining jails, a 68 percent increase in personnel costs. Table 4-1 summarizes new man years and attendant

Table 4-1
Personnel Compliance Costs, Selected Jails[a]

Jail Number	ADP	Current Staff	Personnel Compliance Rate	New Man-Years	Mean Annual Man-Year Cost	Total Additional Staff Cost	Current Annual Personnel Costs	Estimated New Annual Costs
3-1	40	7	67	6.8	12,283	$ 83,524	$ 86,052	$169,576
3-2	53	3.5	71	10.3	8,187	84,326	31,911	116,237
3-3	18	6	82	1.0	13,241	13,241	79,445	92,686
3-4	29	10	70	2.2	10,709	23,560	107,058	130,618
3-5	22	6.5	29	5.2	12,023	62,520	78,148	140,668
3-6	12	1.5	61	3.1	7,086	21,967	10,629	32,596
3-7	20	6	57	6.7	10,882	72,909	65,294	135,203
3-8	25	5.5	65	5.2	10,766	59,213	59,217	118,430
3-9	5	1.5	76	1.1	7,961	8,757	11,942	20,699
Sample totals		47.5		41.6		$430,017	$529,695	$959,713
3-10	65	9	73				$ 89,881	
3-11	28	6.5	86				63,815	
3-12	32	12	74				115,608	
3-13	11	3.5	65				24,626	
3-14	33	8	82	31.7	9,211	$291,989	72,362	$ 820,910
3-15	9	6	79				38,997	
3-16	9	5.5	68				58,068	
3-17	9	2.5	65				22,469	
3-18	7	3	81				27,188	
3-19	4	1.5	76				15,907	
Nonsample totals		57.5		31.7		$291,989	$5,528,921	$ 820,910
Grand totals		104.5		73.3		$722,006	$1,058,616	$1,780,623

[a]Analysis based on data collected and generated by the Correctional Economics Center and interviews with Jail Commission staff, November 1975.

costs; Table 4-2 provides additional detail on the changes standards would occasion in annual and daily costs.

Thirty-four percent more personnel were recommended statewide, for an increase in costs of 28 percent, or $1.7 million. The overwhelming majority of these increases occurred in the smaller jails. Type-4 jails having a median average daily population of five persons, for example, would incur additional personnel costs of $659,735 (an increase of 178 percent), or an average of $36,652 more per jail to comply with the personnel standards alone.

Although it was beyond the scope of the Washington study to examine the efficiency of the small jail unit, the dilemma is apparent. Standards such as those regarding staff sex and surveillance require a minimum staff of 4.5 persons to cover one post twenty-four hours for seven days. For a small jail having one to ten average daily population, the recommended staff may well outnumber inmates. Even though new staff figures are discretionary (a position was not added simply to comply with classification standards), the low average daily populations make the daily costs relatively high. The dramatic increases in personnel costs for the smallest jails reflect the differential impact of the standards and pose serious fiscal questions for small jurisdictions.

Other Operating Costs

For standards other than those with personnel implications, compliance costs were estimated in more individualized ways. Data were available from Jail Commission evaluations about each jail's unique deficiencies in supplies and services. These shortcomings were analyzed in light of the jails' average daily populations and other factors that affected compliance-cost estimation. The techniques used to analyze deficient supplies and services are described below; because the deficiencies themselves were so varied and implied so many different resource requirements, several estimation methods were used.

Supplies. This expenditure category incorporates office and operating supplies and constitutes, on average, 15 percent of total operating costs. Nonpersonnel budget expenditures are not represented similarly from jail to jail due to variation in the way in which goods or services are provided. For example, if a jail prepares its own meals in-house, food costs appear as a component of operating supplies. If meals are catered, the entry may appear as a service expenditure. Many jail budgets lacked detail on components of a particular budget category, so food costs were included here for simplicity.

Office supplies, which consist mostly of paper products and other common office materials, constituted a fairly small component of this category. Again, interviews with Jail Services Commission staff established that the most implications in this category were small (and, indeed, well below the $100 cutoff

Table 4-2
Daily and Annual Personnel Compliance Costs, Selected Jails[a]

Jail Number	Current Annual Unit Costs	New Annual Unit Costs	Increase in Annual Unit Costs	Current Mean Daily Costs	New Mean Daily Costs	Increase in Mean Daily Costs
3-1	$2,151	$ 4,238	$ 2,087	$ 5.89	$ 11.61	$ 5.72
3-2	602	3,725	3,123	1.65	10.21	8.56
3-3	4,414	5,150	736	12.09	14.11	2.02
3-4	3,693	4,504	811	10.12	12.34	2.22
3-5	3,552	6,395	2,843	9.73	17.52	7.79
3-6	886	2,716	1,830	2.43	7.44	5.01
3-7	3,265	6,760	3,495	8.95	18.52	9.57
3-8	2,369	17,174	14,805	6.49	47.05	40.56
3-9	2,388	4,139	1,751	6.54	11.34	4.80
3-10	1,383			3.79		
3-11	2,279			6.24		
3-12	3,540			9.70		
3-13	2,239			6.13		
3-14	2,193	53,786	21,009	6.01	147.35	57.55
3-15	4,333			11.87		
3-16	6,452			17.68		
3-17	2,497			6.84		
3-18	3,884			10.64		
3-19	3,997			10.90		
Overall mean	$2,954	$5,715	$2,763	$ 8.10	$ 15.66	$ 7.59

[a]Analysis based on data collected and generated by the Correctional Economics Center, September-November 1975, and interviews with Jail Commission staff, November 1975.

suggested earlier). For the curious, the "major" new costs would have been for log books and general information forms.

Operating supplies are a catchall for items ranging from bug killer (used in delousing) to plastic bags for clothing storage. Many jails did not provide toilet items such as toothbrushes. Again, these costs would not amount to more than $100 for the average jail.

A more significant component of operating supplies is food. Most of the jails surveyed appeared to have appropriate quantities of food and adequate nutritional quality per serving. However, one standard recommends serving three meals daily. Twenty percent of the jails served only two meals. Commission staff suggested a minimum additional meal cost of sixty cents (the institutional "TV Dinner" cost) as a proxy.[a] In this study the average daily populations of the jails were known, so the cost calculation was straightforward. The nine deficient jails had a total daily population of 124, therefore the statewide daily cost of serving the additional meal would be $75. The annual figure, $27,375, accounted for the major increases in supplies cost.

Health Services. Only 18 percent of the jails provided medical screening and review of records by qualified professionals. Overall care was good, so the major problem appeared to be at the intake stage:

1. Initial screening by jail staff at booking to detect injury or illness
2. Brief medical history obtained at booking for those requiring immediate care
3. Within twelve hours, brief medical history obtained for those *not* requiring immediate care
4. Within forty-eight hours, review and assessment of the medical history by a qualified doctor, nurse, or paramedic

Twelve- and forty-eight-hour requirements made up one standard, so it was impossible to determine directly which of the steps the thirty-six noncompliant jails were skipping.

How service units are calculated and who is hired to deliver them caused significant cost variations. Permitting a doctor, nurse, or paramedic to review medical histories enables a jurisdiction to choose the most efficient service-delivery option. A larger jail, for example, may have on staff a trained paramedic who performs the review as well as duties unrelated to health care. A small jail may use a nurse from the county health department or a local doctor under contract.

The Jail Commission reviewed this standard and recommended thrice-

---

[a]This figure also approximates the "loaded" (staff and raw food) costs of the Department of Social and Health Services for its institutions. The two deficient sample jails did not possess data on food costs.

weekly visits by a contract medical professional. Then it estimated the hours per week that would be required in order to calculate the number of hours for the sample and perform a straight-line extrapolation to the population. The total figure, multiplied by the hourly cost, provided an estimate of compliance. Table 4-3 displays the hours and resultant man years. A lower range estimate for health service delivery may be obtained by using these man years and the statewide annual average salary for correctional officers as a proxy. Application of this technique yielded an estimate of $54,456, which should be regarded as an understatement because additional (paramedical) training would result in higher salaries and no adjustment was made for variations in population turnover rates.

Another approach, and perhaps a more realistic one because admissions are really the relevant group, would be to look at intake and estimate on a per-visit or per-client basis. Total bookings for all jails (excluding the largest, which was not deficient) were estimated at 96,277 for 1974. However, a substantial proportion of these bookings represent persons who did not remain long enough

Table 4-3
Estimates of Medical-Services Man Years[a]

Sample and Extended Sample	
Number of jails	17
Recommended hours/week	83
Hours/year	4316
Man years	208
Average weekly hours/jail	5
Average yearly hours/jail	254
Average man years/jail	0.12
Population	
Number of jails[b]	20
Estimated hours/week	100
Estimated hours/year	5200
Estimated man years	2.5
Totals	
Estimated hours/week	103
Estimated hours/year	9516
Estimated man years	4.57

[a]Analysis based on data collected by and interviews with Jail Commission staff, November 1975.

[b]37 jails do not comply; the sample contains 17 noncompliant jails and 5 compliant; therefore, the number of noncompliant jails in the population is 20.

to be affected by the screening and review standard. The relevant figure, then, is total bookings less these very short-term detainees. It was determined that approximately 55 percent of those booked—an estimated 52,471 persons annually—were placed in pretrial detention for a period exceeding forty-eight hours and therefore should have had medical history reviews. Adjustments for jails in compliance reduced this figure to 41,977.

In fee schedules for nonincarcerated persons, the Department of Social and Health Services reimburses physicians for house calls at a rate of $6.30 per person per visit.[5] This rate results in an estimated upper bound of $264,455— four times the lower bound. This figure was used in the overall cost estimates because it represented the maximum compliance cost for this standard.

Education, Training, and Counseling Services. Forty percent of the jails did not provide opportunities for educational pursuits (such as obtaining a high-school equivalency diploma), vocational training, or general counseling. Costs and enrollment rates for programs provided at a major Washington jail in compliance with these standards resulted in a cost of $48 per participant over a three-month program period.[6] Adjusting for expected enrollments in the deficient jails yielded an estimated prisoner participation figure of 303 persons. Application of the $48 cost on an annual basis resulted in suggested annual education, training, and counseling costs of $58,176.

Adding this cost to the upper-range medical costs produced a $322,631 increase in services expenditures.

Table 4-4 summarizes noncapital compliance costs. The estimated initial annual compliance cost totaled $2 million for the forty-five jails surveyed. This figure, of course, should be considered as a point within a range because regional adjustments were not made, cost increases may occur as a result of inflation, and other cost estimation techniques and methodologies are possible. The basic objective was to derive standards implementation costs based on realistic evaluation of state jail needs and accurate knowledge of current operations and costs.

Table 4-4
Noncapital Compliance Costs

	Total Budget	Personnel	Supplies	Services
Current	$7,727,240	$5,961,841	$1,148,737	$616,662
Increase	$2,011,973	$1,661,967	$27,375	$322,631
Change	26.0%	27.9%	2.4%	52.3%
Total costs at compliance	$9,739,213	$7,623,808	$1,176,112	$939,293

Capital Standards Implementation Costs

General Methodology

Capital costs are those required for construction and improvement of actual jail facilities, as well as for purchase and repair of necessary machinery and equipment. Capital standards compliance costs diverge from other operating costs both in what they represent and in the potentially great costs of their implementation. Building a new facility requires a jurisdiction to amortize the cost over time and would probably necessitate bond issues. The Washington State experience indicates that implementation of even the most costly noncapital operating standards—those with personnel implications—are insignificant in comparison. Standards with capital cost implications comprise only 11 percent of the total standards proposed by the Washington State Jail Commission; however, they are responsible for 95 percent of the total costs of standards implementation. This disproportionate ratio suggests that the Jail Commission was not aware of the potential magnitude of meeting capital standards requirements when it recommended minimum standards.

Of the forty-five jails in Washington, three sets were identified for purposes of capital cost upgrading: those requiring complete rebuilding, those needing major remodeling, and those needing minor remodeling. The needs of each jail were determined from the Jail Commission survey, standards analysis, and individualized case studies utilizing the Jail Commission's familiarity with each facility. Building a new jail was recommended for a jurisdiction whenever the Jail Commission had specified it or when facility remodeling would have been very extensive. The physical additions to plant and equipment necessary to achieve standards compliance and their costs were determined by two architectural firms,[7] both of which had extensive experience designing correctional facilities.

Modifying the Representative Sample Method

As discussed earlier, sampling was used to expedite compliance costs determination; jails were differentiated with respect to jurisdictional size and a random sample was chosen to represent each group. This technique was valuable in deriving compliance costs for certain operations, but it was seriously limited for estimation of capital costs. Jails within a particular population category varied greatly along many dimensions: the specific capital standards with which they were deficient, location in a law enforcement unit, and number and capacity of cells, to indicate only a few differences. Two jails with similar capital deficiency rates might have totally unrelated problems; one might be seriously inadequate in program and recreation areas and in lighting; another might require more cells to eliminate overcrowding. Usage of a sampling technique within any jail type might have resulted in great over- or understatement of capital compliance costs, because for capital costs estimation there were no representative jails.

The technique used to circumvent the sampling problem was a modified case study approach which differed for jails needing replacement and for those requiring either major or minor remodeling. The case study method will be described when the specific methodologies used to derive new and remodeled capital costs are presented.

Assessing Capital Deficiencies of Jails

Jail Commission evaluations had to be supplemented with additional data and preliminarily analyzed before the architectural consultants could approach the problem. This procedure included determining the physical location of each jail and juxtaposing that information with capacity, average daily population, specific Jail Commission recommendations, and capital standards deficiency data. The capital deficiency rate is the ratio of deficient capital standards to all twenty-seven capital standards, expressed as a percentage. This scheme was instrumental in creating an analytical framework for the architectural estimates. Table 4-5 presents an example for eleven jails from the Correctional Economics Center analysis.

To assure that the capital costs estimation was as accurate as possible, it was necessary to carefully determine sizes of the facilities required to meet Washington State's needs. The current needs of each jurisdiction were dictated by utilization and were basic in size determination. Thoughtful planning, however, required anticipation of future needs because of the substantial costs of building new facilities.

Estimation of future jail populations and, by implication, of future capacity needs was attempted by projecting current incarceration patterns. A nonprofit research organization was retained to perform this analysis.[8] Data were collected for 1972 through 1974 and the first half of 1975 about bookings and average daily populations along dimensions of sex, age, misdemeanor versus felony offenses, and pretrial versus sentenced status. The influence of new community programs and changes in criminal justice procedures, such as the repeal of the drunk-in-public statute were also studied.[9] It was determined that the best predictor of short-term jail populations through 1979 was past jail population data.[10] The results of these projections were useful for verification of trends in jurisdictions' jail populations that may affect planning; however, 1979 is too short-term a time horizon for assessing future needs. These projections, therefore, were supplemented with the Jail Commission's expertise about jurisdictions exhibiting significant growth or decrease in jail populations and general statewide population trends data, as well as current utilization data.

Uncertainty Inherent in Cost Estimates

Although the case study approach included as much individuation as possible for each jurisdiction, the results are rather general. Time and resource constraints upon any research endeavor, combined here with the Jail Commission's requirements for this analysis, demanded a degree of specificity that suggested a potential magnitude for standards compliance costs. For capital costs, especially, the estimates are in all likelihood a maximum cost figure and one that could be modified by individual jurisdictions. For example, a small facility might use a multipurpose room for recreational and educational activities (a practice allowed by the standards), as well as medical examinations. Such sharing of core facilities would reduce the required capital expenditures for compliance. Local decisions may also affect actual implementation costs in other ways. Although projections of jail populations have implications for location of new facilities within counties and consolidation of jurisdictions with low projected utilizations, the highly political nature of these decisions requires that they be left to legislative or local jurisdictional discretion. The capital cost estimates provided here assume that each facility for which Jail Commission surveys indicated substantial deficiencies will be replaced or remodeled. Elimination of certain jails and consolidation of two counties or a county facility and a city facility might be more feasible. This consideration, as well as the variety of choices available to an individual jurisdiction in determining exactly how capital standards compliance will be achieved, suggests that the estimates provided herein are the upper end point in a range of possible capital standards compliance costs.

Estimation of New Capital Costs

As a result of the standards evaluations, the Jail Commission recommended rebuilding seventeen jails to achieve compliance with capital standards. The capacities of these jails ranged from 10 to 62 and two exceeded capacity; for these substantially larger capacities have been recommended. These jails were sorted into four groups according to their current average daily populations and capacities and their projected needs. The groups did not correspond to the four jail types used in the rest of the analysis. Four architectural design plans were developed. The size or intended capacity of each of these designs was based upon the average of the projected capacities required for each group. The largest facility in the state, which had a capacity of approximately 750, required new building and substantial remodeling, and it was treated separately because of its unique needs.

The architectural consultants structured the four designs for cost estimates so that they could be adapted to the individual requirements of each jurisdiction requiring a new jail. Differences in jail size due to variations in jurisdictional needs, however, require using a range of sizes to estimate construction costs

66

Table 4-5
Description of Jail Facilities[a]

Jail Number	Location	Capacity	Average Daily Population	Capital Deficiency Rate	Recommended Improvements	Cells	Dorms	Dayrooms
1.	City hall/top	750	622	18.9	Major remodel	x	x	
2.	City hall/top	420	332	15.4	None			
3.	Courthouse/4th	196	96	61.5	Major remodel	x		x
4.	Courthouse and City hall/5th	159	55	92.0	Remodel/ new	x	x	x
5.	City hall/3rd	150	47	12.0	Minor remodel			
6.	Wing	148	100	58.3	Major remodel	x	x	x
7.	Courthouse/5th	142	64	38.5	Minor remodel	x	x	x
8.	Courthouse/2nd	101	35	3.7	None			
9.	Courthouse/top 3rd	80	33	16.0	Major remodel	x	x	x
10.	Courthouse/top 3rd	66	29	45.8	Major remodel	x		x
11.	Courthouse/top	62	53	62.9	New			

[a]All data collected and generated by the Correctional Economics Center and the Washington State City and County Jail Commission; data analysis prepared by the Economics Center.

because scale economies affect average costs per bed. Almost all functional areas in a jail vary with size; large institutions require not only more cells but also larger booking areas, kitchen facilities, and more visiting areas. Within certain size ranges, however, most of the supportive areas—those required for booking, food preparation, laundry services, and recreation—remain constant, although inmate housing needs vary. Scale economies may emerge when jails of different sizes are compared, particularly for inmate housing. The reason, in part, is that in smaller jails separate cells must be built for each bed to meet standards requiring segregation of inmates by classification. Costs of additional security devices, grillwork, plumbing, and so on will increase these per-bed costs. In a jail large enough to utilize dormitories for particular classifications, per-bed housing costs will probably decrease.

In Washington State, the architectural cost estimates for new construction

Lavatory	Showers	Isolation	Recreation	Education	Library	Kitchen	Medical	Visiting	Laundry	Storage	Offices	Booking	Lighting	Emer Power	Water	Heat	Ventilation	Air Conditioning
X	X									X			X					
X	X	X						X	X	X		X	X				X	
X	X	X	X	X		X		X	X	X	X	X	X	X	X	X	X	X
			X	X			X	X					X				X	
X	X	X	X	X		X		X	X		X	X	X					
X	X									X	X	X	X				X	
X	X	X					X	X										
X	X		X	X	X			X	X		X	X	X					

exhibited scale economies for housing, administration, and intake and visiting functions. Administration and intake areas require costly surveillance and security equipment, including a control room, which must be present regardless of a jail's capacity. Visiting areas require increments in square footage beyond a basic "core" area that would service a small number of inmates, with concomitant per-bed cost reductions. Table 4-6 shows three functional areas for five jails of increasing capacities and their per-bed average and diminishing costs for each functional area. In determining the size jails for which capital cost estimates were required, the interaction of two factors was considered. The first was the size at which all functional areas in a jail, both inmate housing and supportive areas, must increase to serve larger populations. The second was the size of jails in Washington State that needed to be rebuilt. It was determined that jail design capacities of 15, 32, 55, and 100 would be most useful.

Table 4-6
Cost Diminutions for Increasing Capacities, New Construction[a]

Per-bed Cost for Capacity of	Housing	Functional Area: Administration/ Intake	Visiting Area
15	$12,982	$4,070	$1,352
32	12,002	2,054	990
55	9,599	1,453	774
100	8,227	1,773[b]	567
153	7,936	840	464
Cost Differences Between Capacities of			
15-32	$980 (7.5%)	$2,016 (49.5%)	$362 (26.8%)
32-55	2,403 (20.0%)	601 (29.3%)	216 (21.8%)
55-100	1,372 (14.3%)	−320 (−22.0%)	207 (26.7%)
100-153	291 (3.5%)	933 (52.6%)	103 (18.2%)
15-153	5,046 (38.0%)	$3,230 (79.4)	$888 (65.7%)

[a]Cost estimates for new construction capacities of 15, 32, 55, and 153 prepared by Gordon Ruehl; report submitted to the Correctional Economics Center, 26 November 1975. For capacity of 100, cost estimates are from Carl Easters, "Architectural Cost Analysis, Projected Detention Facility for Thurston County, Washington"; memorandum dated 13 November 1975.

[b]This estimate included some administrative cost components not included in those for other capacities, causing it to be disproportionately high.

For analytical purposes, blueprints for new jails are not necessary; square footage estimates and costs by functional area are. These designs, however, are more abstract than final blueprints created after extensive feasibility research. For this reason, certain design plans used to derive cost estimates include an allowance for "nonassignable space," which compensates for placement of walls, hall space, walkway variations, and other elements that may only be known with certainty when a plan specific to a jurisdiction's needs is prepared. A contingency factor may also be included to allow for unforeseen difficulties during building (for example, extraordinary site preparation). The question of specific jail characteristics with respect to technological innovations and programmatic design is not addressed here because local jurisdictional input is required for such decisions.

The difficulties of assigning costs to seventeen new jails were magnified by the need to anticipate the physical location of jail facilities. Most county and city jails are located in courthouses or city halls. It would not have been realistic to design entire new county or municipal buildings for this analysis. Consequently, it was assumed that new jails would be built as freestanding entities or possibly as totally self-contained extensions to existing local governmental buildings. The jail designs from which the capital cost estimates were derived are for separate buildings, and include the sheriffs' departments. For most jurisdictions in Washington State, law enforcement (sheriffs' or police departments) and jail facilities are housed together, and it may be assumed that this situation will continue. Law enforcement building costs, however, are not indicated in the estimates presented here.

The format used to estimate new capital costs is presented in Appendix F, which lists the eight main cost-center functions in the architectural consultants' schema for a new jail constructed for a population of one hundred. Cost components are differentiated with respect to both functional area and type of construction or equipment cost. The total cost of particular jail functions, as well as individual building components (for example, special equipment), is discernible, as are the percentage distributions of these costs within a jail. This scheme permits a convenient method for assessing why costs within a jail vary: maximum security areas for felon populations necessitate more costly surveillance equipment; kitchen appliances are needed for food preparation; booking and control areas may require specialized sight and sound monitoring devices. Representative housing costs for minimum security inmates (either men or women) would be $49 per square foot; by comparison, a new screening and evaluation room would cost approximately $62 per square foot. The latter is more costly because medical apparatus is needed to equip the room and more specialized electrical and plumbing systems might need to be installed. The percentage distributions indicate that inmate housing accounts for nearly 60 percent of all jail costs, jail administration for 13 percent, and food service for 11 percent. All costs are in 1975 dollars and reflect the current and historical construction markets in Washington State. Architectural fees and state sales tax are included, but not the costs of site acquisition and preparation, and outside public utilities. These costs would increase the total by an estimated 12 to 13 percent.

The cost estimates for new capital are presented in Table 4-7; they include costs for each replacement capacity group, per-bed costs for new construction, and total costs. By specifying these within a group, new building costs are not attributable to any particular jurisdiction within that group. This situation is desirable because actual building costs, even for those jails with similar capacities, will vary when each locality's unique characteristics are considered; also, the Jail Commission was not concerned with the costs of specific jails. The total cost of $19.6 million is, of course, a point estimate intended to facilitate planning by the Washington State Legislature and is not a measure of what the state and localities will actually spend in any given year. Even if the state were to decide that building seventeen new local jails is a priority, a method would have to be devised for financing and amortizing these costs.

The replacement design capacities range from fifteen to one hundred. As the

Table 4-7
New Capital-Construction Costs[a]

Group	Replacement Design Capacity	Average Cost/ New Facility	Per-bed Costs	Total Cost/ Group
1	100	$1,908,027	$19,080	$3,816,054
2	55	1,270,696	23,104	8,894,872
3	32	959,795	29,994	5,758,769
4	15	565,726	37,715	1,131,452
Total				$19,601,147[b]
Average per-bed cost			$24,289	

[a]Analysis performed by the Correctional Economics Center, based upon new capital cost estimates by Gordon Ruehl and Carl Easters; memoranda to the Economics Center, November-December 1975.

[b]AIA fees are estimated on a sliding scale of 8.0 to 8.5 percent depending on design capacity; also includes Washington State sales tax of 5 percent.

design capacity decreases from one hundred to fifteen, per-bed costs increase nearly 11 percent. The higher cost for new construction at smaller capacities helps shift the average per-bed cost statewide for new construction upward to $24,289. This figure poses serious considerations for planning and suggests that the cost of local jurisdictional control may be prohibitive.

Estimation of Remodeling Costs

With few exceptions, Jail Commission inspections resulted in recommendations for rebuilding or remodeling every jail in the state. A total of twenty-six jails became candidates for remodeling; thirteen required major work and thirteen minor alterations. Again, a sample was selected and case studies developed. The deficient jails were grouped by capacity. Average daily populations and utilization data were also used to assure that the jail capacities used for remodeling were sufficient; for example, a jail with a capacity of 50 but an average daily population of 10 might warrant less ambitious improvements. Five size classes were derived and a representative jail selected from each. For example, the five jails in the largest category had capacities ranging from 142 to 196 but ADPs of 47 to 135. The jail selected for analysis had a capacity of 159 and was also representative of the capital deficiencies of that class. Other representative jails had capacities of 61, 40, 22, and 5. Each sample jail was analyzed by a correctional architect and the costs for remodeling each subelement of the capital standards were estimated. This process was performed for each standard for which a deficiency existed for any jail within that type, regardless of whether the sample jail was in compliance. The resultant cost figures for living quarters, program space, booking, and other areas were then individually applied to each jail in the group according to its deficiencies. In other words, even though the model jail might be deficient in, for example, recreation space, this cost was not entered across the board for all jails in the group, but only for those jails specifically found deficient in that area.

As was the case with new capital construction, certain subelement costs do not change linearly with jail size. Table 4-8 displays the remodeling costs for deficient capital areas. In housing, for example, the requirement for segregation of prisoners necessitates single-cell construction for smaller jails. Dormitory accommodations can only be considered with the second design capacity of 22. For the smaller jails housing costs were a much smaller fraction of total remodeling costs (28 versus 83 percent for the largest jails). Total program areas (in square feet) and costs increased as jail size increased; however, unit costs decreased for larger jails. For example the cost of multipurpose/educational space (144 square feet) in the smallest jails was $6260. For jails with capacities of 22, this space increases to 300 square feet for a cost of $13,300. The largest design capacity includes 730 square feet at $31,700. The per-inmate construction costs decline from $1252 to $199, with similar results occurring in other areas. Per-inmate visiting room costs decrease from $640 to $426 for the largest jails. However, as jail size increases, more differentiated space is assigned to some subelements (such as more special-purpose rooms) and the total cost per client for such areas may actually rise. This phenomenon occurs with medical facilities, laundry, offices, and booking areas. The latter area was one requiring rebuilding in many jails. The standards called for "safe and secure" booking areas and also recommended holding cells, search rooms, and identification areas. For the very small jail, complying with this standard involves substantial cost. A complete monitoring and surveillance system, for example, would cost $20,800 ($52,000 for the largest jails). Adding this to the cost of other recommended improvements would result in a cost of $55,700 for new booking areas in jails with capacities of 5 to 22. By comparison, this cost is only tripled ($157,400) for a jail with capacity of 159.

Summary statistics for remodeling costs appear in Table 4-9. It lists the costs attendant to raising all jails to compliance with only those standards for which they were deficient; the costs are specific to the major or minor remodeling recommendations of the Jail Commission. Jails were assumed to require design capacities that were similar to or slightly greater than their present capacities. The "average" remodeling cost would be $1.6 million for a type-2 jail, $500,000 for type-3 jails, and $36,000 for type-4 jails. The last group consists of facilities so small that certain physical areas were considered too large or expensive to construct; substitute arrangements include sending inmates to a local hospital rather than maintaining an infirmary. The largest jail was a special case and warranted an estimate unique to that facility. New design capacity

Table 4-8
Remodeling Costs for Capital Deficiencies, Selected Jail Capacities[a]

Standard Capital Unit	Capacity = 5			Capacity = 22			Capacity = 40			Capacity = 61			Capacity = 159		
	Square Feet	Total Cost	Cost/ Inmate	Square Feet	Total Cost	Cost/ Inmate	Square Feet	Total Cost	Cost/ Inmate	Square Feet	Total Cost	Cost/ Inmate	Square Feet	Total Cost	Cost/ Inmate
Recreation	150	$6,800	$1360	N/A	—	—	750	$35,750	$894	800	$34,500	$566	800	$34,500	$217
Education	144	6,260	1252	300	$13,300	$605	400	19,000	475	500	22,500	369	730	31,700	199
Library	80	3,700	740	100	5,000	227	300	18,700	468	350	19,400	318	N/A	—	—
Feeding	200	13,000	2600	N/A	—	—	530	53,300	1333	450	68,000	1115	1398	141,920	893
Medical	N/A	—	—	80	8,727	397	250	18,717	468	230	17,227	282	230	17,727	111
Visiting	80	3,200	640	80	3,200	145	684[b]	23,277	582	860[c]	38,900	637	1485[d]	67,776	426
Laundry	N/A	—	—	N/A	—	—	220	15,300	383	325	21,050	345	505	31,000	195
Inmate storage	N/A	—	—	N/A	—	—	120	4,560	114	100	4,350	71	150	7,500	47
Offices	300	12,000	2400	300	12,000	545				500	20,500	336	500	20,500	129
Booking/release	510	34,900	6980	580	59,500	2705	1095	81,120	2028	1095	66,800	1095	1960	168,400	1059

[a]Analysis performed by the Correctional Economics Center based on remodeling costs estimated by Carl Easters and Gordon Ruehl; memoranda to the Economics Center, November-December 1975. Costs include demolition, basic structures, special equipment, and mechanical and electrical installations. An entry of N/A indicates either that a jail was too small to warrant the area or that no jails were deficient.

[b]At capacity of and above 40, waiting rooms and visitor counters are added to basic visiting space.

[c]Incorporates visiting space of 65 square feet/inmate for 8 inmates.

[d]Incorporates visiting space of 65 square feet/inmate for 19 inmates.

Table 4-9
Remodeling Cost Estimates for Twenty-six Jails[a]

Standard No.	Short Title	Type 1 (N = 1)	Type 2 (N = 5)	Type 3 (N = 7)	Type 4 (N = 13)	Standard Total
102	Quarters		$6,693,536	$2,525,841	$132,116	$ 9,351,493
103	Cells/dorms		95,000	98,500	6,800	200,300
104	Recreation		86,600	110,850	25,040	222,490
105	Education		0	42,900	14,800	57,700
106	Library		254,000	121,300	13,000	388,300
107	Feeding		8,500	36,467	0	44,967
109	Medical (general)		8,727	26,921	8,727	44,375
111	Medical isolation		200,500	98,455	29,300	328,255
112	Visiting (general)		12,800	13,822	12,800	39,422
113	Visiting (confidential)		104,800	52,850	0	157,650
114	Laundry		30,000	8,910	0	38,910
115	Inmate storage		54,500	45,200	36,000	135,700
116	Offices		517,200	276,380	125,200	918,780
117	Booking/release		0	20,000	60,000	80,000
118	Emergency power					
	Total	$10,044,700	$8,066,163	$3,478,396	$463,783	$22,053,042
	AIA Fees and Washington State sales tax[b]					2,866,895
	Grand Total					$24,919,937

[a] Analysis performed by the Correctional Economics Center based upon remodeling cost estimates by Carl Easters and Gordon Ruehl; memoranda to the Economics Center, November-December 1975.

[b] AIA fees are estimated on a sliding scale; 8 percent was selected for reference; also includes Washington State sales tax of 5 percent.

totaled 1065 beds and approximately $10 million in capital improvements was estimated, primarily for living quarters.

In addition to the forty-three facilities for which the costs of capital upgrading were estimated, there were four jurisdictions that required new jails to achieve standards compliance. The Jail Commission, however, did not perform standards evaluations for these jails because they were condemned or were to be used only as short-term holding facilities or because in one case it was determined that a new jail was necessary without performing an actual evaluation. No standards evaluation was done for one county that had already planned a new facility. Although it is impossible to determine the noncapital improvement costs for these facilities, an estimate for building four new jails is included here to complete the discussion on capital cost compliance. For the four small jurisdictions, a total capital cost of $2.57 million was calculated, based on new design capacities of fifteen.

Capital Costs Summary

The total cost of building seventeen new jails and remodeling the twenty-six requiring major or minor improvements is estimated at $44,521,084.[b] Because the estimates allow for growth in incarcerated populations and compliance with all standards related to physical plant improvement, the investment cost per inmate at present population levels is $23,519. Although capital acquisitions are one-time expenditures, they should be part of annual operating costs because they are used over time; complete cost accounting must include an amount for their yearly usage. To suggest a realistic annual figure for planning purposes by the state legislature and local decision maker, the total cost estimated here was amortized at 10 percent.[c] This rate yields an estimated increase of $4.45 million in annual operating costs for capital expenditures. When finalized, these amounts should also reflect site acquisition costs, outside public utilities usage, extraordinary inflation, and local interest rates.

These estimates, however approximate, indicate the magnitude of expenditures required to attain capital standards compliance and raise important questions for decision makers regarding the cost effectiveness of maintaining

[b]If the four jurisdictions for which the Jail Commission did not perform routine evaluations are included, the total reaches $47,089,480. The $44.5 million was used here because the "workplan" specified that jail evaluations were to be the basis for estimating upgrading costs.
[c]This note is based on borrowing rates ranging from 7 to 9 percent for most states, an amortization factor, and a small margin of uncertainty. Over 30 years, an 8 percent interest rate would result in $17 million in interest charges on a $10 million institution; therefore, the total cost is approximately $27 million over 30 years, or roughly $1 million per year. (See Neil M. Singer and Virginia B. Wright, *Cost Analysis of Correctional Standards: Institutional-Based Programs and Parole* [Washington, D.C.: Correctional Economics Center, 1975]).

forty-five separate jails of the size variation found in Washington State. Particularly if the state is to consider assistance in funding to local jurisdictions, such issues need to be addressed.

Summary

Operating, new facility, and remodeling cost estimates each required a unique methodology. Standards first were grouped into functional areas. Within each area, specific deficiencies were identified from the compliance ratings made by the Jail Commission. Attention then was focused even more narrowly on standards requiring more than $100 to implement. At this juncture, the challenge was to find and decide on the best sources of cost information. Special studies were undertaken by architectural experts to estimate the cost of new facilities and to identify the factors internal to a jail that accounted for variations in per-bed construction costs for capacities of 15, 32, 55, and 100. Replacing the seventeen institutions to meet standards would require an estimated $19.6 million. Major or minor remodeling of twenty-six other jails would take another $24.9 million for only the areas found deficient. Both estimates, adjusted for scale of operation, derive from and are a consequence of specific standards requiring visiting space, medical examining rooms, booking areas, multipurpose rooms, and so on.

Staff, supplies, and purchased services would add another $2 million allocated to such functions as health care, surveillance, prisoner classification, and staff training.

The total bill—$46.5 million—would be substantial and beyond the means of most local governments. Yet the standards, per se, are not unrealistic. They represent a competent statement of modern practice. This acknowledgement, coupled with fiscal realities, forces policy makers to decide who should pay.

Notes

1. National Sheriffs' Association, "Determining Needs for Staff," *Handbook on Jail Administration* (Washington, D.C.: National Sheriffs' Association, 1974), pp. 16-18 (hereafter National Sheriffs' Association). Holidays, annual and sick leave are taken into account.

2. Standards and Goals, p. 494. See also National Sheriffs' Association, pp. 34-35.

3. See United States Bureau of Prisons, *Jail Operations: A Training Course for Jail Officers* (Washington, D.C.: Government Printing Office, n.d.).

4. Interview with Jail Services Commission staff, 21 November 1975.

5. Washington State Department of Social and Health Services, *Schedule*

of Maximum Allowances and Program Descriptions was used for these calculations.

6. Seattle Central Community College, *Progress Report*, 14 August 1975. Law and Justice Planning Office Grant #1521.

7. The firms that were retained by the Washington State City and County Jail Commission were Bennett, Johnson, Selenes and Smith, Olympia, Washington; and Walker/McGough/Foltz/Lyerla, Architects and Engineers, Spokane, Washington. Cost estimates were prepared as memoranda to the Correctional Economics Center during November-December 1975.

8. Battelle Northwest Law and Justice Study Center, in-house report to the Correctional Economics Center, November 1975.

9. Ibid., p. 3.

10. Ibid., p. 8.

5 State and Local Cost Sharing

Given a state commitment to the upgrading of county and other local level institutions, some form of subsidy from the state to local governmental units may be deemed appropriate. A subsidy is offered to public and private entities in order to elicit a behavior: by providing a subsidy, the grantor decreases the cost to the grantee of acting in the manner (or producing the output) desired by the grantor. Such policies are evident throughout the U.S. economy.

Public sector subsidies include state grants to local school districts that are contingent on certain actions by the local school authorities. Federal revenue sharing is yet another form of subsidy, one that reflects the federal government's desire to increase the volume of government services rendered locally (and incorporates the provision that the revenue sharing funds may not be used to decrease local taxes).

Private sector subsidies, that is, transfers from the public to the private sector, are also widespread. The construction of industrial parks by localities and the granting of tax holidays for companies moving into the parks are practices by which local governments attempt to attract industry and involve a subsidy from that government to the manufacturer who locates in the community. In order to stimulate shipbuilding in the United States, the U.S. Maritime Administration has subsidized the construction of new merchant vessels in domestic shipyards, thus providing funds to private shipbuilders (or allowing private shipowners to acquire American ships at a price below that prevailing in the open market).

The longest-standing subsidy arrangement in criminal justice is the California Probation Subsidy. Dating from 1965, the subsidy plan provides financial aid to the counties in the state that reduce state commitments from their jurisdictions below some targeted level.[1] The subsidy is performance based so it rises with the percentage reduction in state commitments from the base rate established prior to a county entering the program. Moreover, a standard of performance is expected: not only must the commitment level from a county fall in order for it to be eligible for funds, but the county also must provide supervision services to probationers at an approved level in order to receive reimbursement. A similar program to generate higher local level corrections effort has been initiated in Minnesota, and the general trend towards providing subsidies to increase local effort in the criminal justice arena is reflected in the LEAA program of block grants to local planning agencies to pursue the development of local programs to solve local problems.

Ample precedent exists, therefore, for a plan of state subsidization of local effort. The question that arises for the state of Washington, then, is how the subsidy will be determined: the conditions of eligibility and the differential volume of subsidy provided to different counties. Three basic criteria may be identified as the principles that should guide a state subsidy program: equity, efficiency, and efficacy. Each implies a different distributional pattern for subsidy payments, and we must therefore examine them both in isolation and in interaction. We will first review the elements in order.

The federal revenue sharing program allocation formula, with respect to general revenue sharing at least is focused wholly on the issue of the fairness of disbursements. The allocation formula considers "fiscal capacity," a measure of the relative affluence (and thus relative taxability) of a potential recipient jurisdiction, along with "relative effort," or the current level of taxation in that jurisdiction compared to others of comparable capacity. These considerations of equity remain salient for state disbursements to counties, so we will examine in the first section below the current pattern of federal general revenue cash flows to counties in Washington. These findings illustrate the allocational formulas that would be appropriate for general disbursement by the state to its constituent counties. However, Washington's "revenue sharing" is directed at the upgrading of a particular set of government services, namely, those rendered in correctional institutions, so a closer examination of the impact of such disbursements on the quality of jails is warranted.

If funds are provided to counties as a function of their current demonstrated "need," for augmentation of local budgets, then extreme inefficiency in corrections service provision would in no way affect disbursements. Consider the following example. County Able and County Baker have identical fiscal capacities, but County Able has a higher exhibited level of relative tax effort than does County Baker. Simultaneously, County Able spends three times the dollars per inmate day on correctional institution services that County Baker expends, but despite higher expenditures, it is no closer to meeting the standards for "ideal" jails. Based on equity alone, the state would provide more money to County Able than to County Baker because the former is taxing itself more heavily than is the latter. However, we know that County Baker is more efficient than County Able (and this difference in ability to get results with given amounts of money may explain County Baker's lower level of tax effort). Thus, application of the federal allocation scheme may serve simply to reward locally financed inefficiency.

Factors other than relative fiscal effort and capacity must be taken into consideration for efficiency to be served by state allocations to counties. These elements are discussed in the second section below, where we review the different attainments and relative efforts and efficiencies of the local jails of the state of Washington. Introduction of a mix of equity and efficiency criteria may thus make possible a system of subsidies that optimally produces the results desired by the state.

Given the state's commitment to improved correctional facilities, it does not logically follow that the optimal subsidy program is the optimal method by which those state ends might be attained. It may be far more appropriate for a state simply to legislate the minimal acceptable conditions under which persons may be incarcerated and to provide for inspection and enforcement of state standards. If, however, the state commitment to upgrading county jails includes a simultaneous commitment to local self-determination, then a subsidy program may be a viable tool. A range of issues regarding the "strings" attached to such subsidy disbursements remain, however, and these are addressed in the third section of this chapter, along with the use of a corrections quality or "efficacy" measure as an element in the allocation formula that might produce the required incentives.

The interactions of these three principles and the possible objective of a subsidy program require further examination, because adoption of a basis for equitable distribution may undermine the extent to which a subsidy can serve to promote efficacy or efficiency. In the fourth section below, then, we address problems of interaction and the bases along which the grantor—in this case the state of Washington—may translate its available funds and its hierarchy of corrections objectives into an appropriate per-capita subsidy to its counties.

As noted in preceding chapters, conformance to the standards of the National Commission may well require major capital construction, in addition to increased operations budgets. The discussion in the main body of this chapter is devoted exclusively to the matter of ongoing subsidies. A brief appendix addressed to capital cost considerations is included because this problem, although simpler in many ways than that of the ongoing relationship between counties and the state, cannot be ignored.

Equity Considerations in Subsidies

It is a commonly accepted dictum that subsidy formulas that fail to account for variations in needs and requirements deriving from the population sizes of recipient jurisdictions are unfair. Thus, disbursement procedures that grant the same amount of money to, say, a county with 250,000 people and a county with 50,000 residents would be inappropriate and inequitable.

The first principle of equity is thus that each person should count equally in the formula, other things being equal. This analogy to the one-man-one-vote principle assumes, however, that the per-person needs and relative efforts of different localities are roughly comparable. When this assumption is invalid in application, the simple formula must be modified. Three critical characteristics of persons in political subdivisions have routinely been employed as bases for deviating from the equal-shares-per-person formula: income per capita, taxes paid locally per capita, and assessed property valuation per capita. These measures reflect affluence and poverty in an area, as well as the extent to which the people in a jurisdiction are willing to tax themselves for local government services provision.

The principle of progressive taxation embodied in the federal personal income tax argues that the more a person has, the more she or he can afford to pay in taxes. Thus, in addressing revenue sharing or other disbursements from a central government to constituent jurisdictions, some consideration is given to *income* per capita. The lower the local income per person, it is held, the less money a county can equitably raise in taxes. Thus, the tax collections are expected to be lower in poorer counties. However, the differences in collections that exist in the various counties do not correspond precisely to differences in per-person incomes. This fact emerges from the different levels of "tax effort" exhibited in different areas, frequently measured as *tax collections per capita.* If all property were owned by the persons residing on or working therein, these two variables would suffice to describe taxable capacity and fiscal effort. However, commercial and industrial property is often not locally owned. A major divergence between the real estate *assessed valuations per capita* and local incomes may thus be present, if valuable property present in the county is not reflected in the average income for the county residents due to absentee ownership.

Table 5-1 examines tax collections, valuations, and incomes per capita for selected counties in Washington and some of the relationships among these three measures. Apparent tax burden relative to taxable capacity varies widely, depending on the measures one employs, as this table demonstrates. Moreover, variety is the keyword for the counties of Washington, where, for example, the per-capita income of County A nears $4500 and that of County G falls below $2900. Some explanation of the extreme ranges are, therefore, in order because some measure of capacity and effort must be incorporated into an equitable subsidy for upgrading local correctional institutions.

We have three measures of the burden of taxation: the tax collection per capita (column 1), which ranges from a high of almost $400 to a low of barely $100; the collections as a percentage of income (column 4), ranging from 3 percent up to 10 percent; and taxes relative to assessed property values (column 5), which run from a low of 0.68 percent to a peak of almost 2.0 percent. Depending on which measure is employed, the analyst attempting to assess tax effort can come to vastly different conclusions. We can associate each measure with a different interpretation of the relevance and significance of taxation.

Taxes per capita describe the burden relative to the pure standard that "all men are . . . equal." The implication of this standard is that the ideal tax is the one that affects all persons equally.

Taxes per unit income is a measure that reinserts the critical verb in the standards used above ("all men are *created* equal") and recognizes that not all may have *achieved* equally. This standard argues that those who have benefited

Table 5-1
Equity Measures Computation: Selected Washington Counties

County	1 Tax Collections Per Capita (1972)	2 Property Valuation Per Capita (1973)	3 Income Per Capita (1972)	4 Tax/Income (1/3)	5 Tax/Valuation (1/2)	6 Income/Valuation (3/2)	7 Income-Valuation Index	8 Tax Effort Index
A	$247.25	$12,398	$4,493	0.055	0.0199	0.362	1.392	77
B	$123.68	$9,960	$3,899	0.032	0.0124	0.391	1.504	48
C	111.79	8,666	3,572	0.031	0.0129	0.412	1.585	49
D	125.99	9,946	3,063	0.041	0.0127	0.308	1.185	49
E	$120.60	$12,220	$3,809	0.032	0.0099	0.312	1.200	38
F	$295.57	$21,638	$3,515	0.084	0.0137	0.162	0.623	52
G	120.57	11,184	2,876	0.042	0.0108	0.257	0.988	41
H	288.32	21,186	3,391	0.088	0.0122	0.138	0.531	47
J	102.23	8,448	3,375	0.030	0.0121	0.399	1.535	46
K	357.36	29,935	4,032	0.088	0.0119	0.125	0.519	46
L	393.98	57,694	3,806	0.103	0.0068	0.066	0.254	26
Average, all counties	$197.43	$15,487	$3,518	0.054	0.0134	0.270	1.000	52

the most from this society (and earn the highest incomes) can return to society more than can those who have attained less.

Taxes per assessed valuation implicitly assumes that the predominant local tax is the real estate levy and that the value of real estate in a county reflects the affluence in that area. This measure assumes that the value of the real property in a county indicates the capacity of persons living in that jurisdiction to pay taxes.

The counties selected in Table 5-1 provide excellent examples of the inadequacy of all these measures. Taken individually, County L, for example, has tax collections roughly double the average for Washington counties, yet its assessed valuation is almost four times the state average and its income is only 8 percent above the mean. Taxes could clearly be levied on the owners of extremely valuable property in the county. These individuals would still not be heavily burdened because taxes as a percentage of real estate value are lower in County L than any place else in the state. However, if the very heavy tax burden does fall on actual residents of the county (who might very well not own the valuable real estate), then the local tax burden would be extremely high relative to incomes. Because we do not know what the tax incidence really is, employing exclusively the per-capita tax, tax per income, or tax per valuation would provide us with a distorted picture.

Another case in point is County J, an area with slightly below average incomes, but miniscule per-capita assessed valuations on property and a per-capita tax collection of barely over half the state average. It is possible that the county does not need to collect heavier taxes to deliver the services expected by its residents and should not, therefore, be faulted for its extremely low tax yield. The county tax collections as a proportion of its assessed valuation in fact are over 90 percent of the state average. Once again, we find that the taxation/income ratio would tend to distort the actual facts of relative efforts at providing public services, and some adjustment is necessary.

One possible adjustment factor is an index value for each county of the ratio of income to property (column 7). This figure reflects the capacity of county residents to realize incomes from the property in their county, relative to state average capacities. As we would suspect for the two counties we have just examined, the residents of County L do relatively poorly, realizing a mere 26 percent of the statewide average returns on their property. On the other hand, the people living in County J do exceptionally well, and their incomes demonstrate a capacity to earn from the existing valuation on property, which is over 50 percent above the state average.

If we adjust the "pure" ability-to-pay fiscal effort measure (taxation as a percentage of income) for the income extraction capability index (ratio of per-capita income to per-capita valuation), we produce a net measure of taxation effort. This measure is primarily based on income per capita, but it recognizes the presence in many counties of industrial and commercial development (not always reflected in local incomes) and penalizes those counties not placing a major tax burden on such income-generating property. The tax effort index is one thousand times the product of the income-valuation index and the tax/income ratio. Under this adjusted measure, County J has a net tax effort index of 46 and County L has an index of 26.

Table 5-2 summarizes the equity assessments inherent in the three scales we have considered. This format is one we use repeatedly below as a vehicle for summarizing the impact on distributions of different relative measures when a choice of allocation tools is available. We thus present a detailed explanation of the format here and assume that further repetition of the interpretive process is not necessary when this format is repeated.

First, if Table 5-2 is to have any value to the analyst, it must be interpreted under strict *ceteris paribus* conditions; that is, the allocation shares associated with the three different equity measures must be judged, and one selected, under the assumption that all other variables that might affect allocations have equal value for all counties. In this instance, then, we assume that population size, efficiency of corrections quality production, and efficacy of county-based corrections are constant across all counties in the state of Washington. The table displays the range, that is, the high, mean, and low values for the measure, along with the ratio of the top of the scale to the bottom. Policy makers may want to have a broader or narrower range depending on the degree of discrimination on

Table 5-2
Distributional Characteristics of Equity Scales[a]

	E1 Tax/Income	E2 Tax/Valuation	E3 Index of Tax/Income
Range of Indexed Values			
High value	1.91	1.49	1.48
Mean value	1.00	1.00	1.00
Low value	0.56	0.51	0.45
(High value)/low value)	3.41	2.92	3.29
Percentage Allocation Shares			
Top jurisdiction	4.9%	3.8%	3.8%
Top 5 jurisdictions	20.9	17.2	13.7
Mean jurisdiction	2.6	2.6	2.6
Low 5 jurisdictions	7.7	9.1	9.1
Low jurisdiction	1.4	1.3	1.3
Top minus low	3.5	2.5	3.1
Top 5 minus low 5	13.2	15.9	4.6

[a]All scales normalized to show mean value of 1.00.

the basis of equity intended. The table also contains the percentage allocation shares for the county and the five top and five bottom counties. These measures tell us how much of any subsidy monies would go to each county on a per-capita basis if the units were identical in all aspects other than the dimension being measured.

Looking specifically at Table 5-2, we find that the ranges of E1 and E3 are comparable but E2 moves through a slightly narrower range. When we look at percentage allocations, however, we find that measure E1 would create the greatest disparity between the counties, whereas measure E3 would produce the least. (This last conclusion derives from the 13.7 percent for the top five counties and the 9.1 percent for the bottom five, the difference between which is only 4.6 percent.) However, measure E2 may be preferable to E3 if low disparity is desirable, because its top value is only 2.5 percent above its low value. Criticism of the federal general revenue sharing has focused on the fact that income alone does not adequately define taxable capacity, but no single variable may be able to do so unless it incorporates some measure of the extent of poverty and wealth in a local jurisdiction. Inclusion of the income extraction capability index used to compute equity scale E3 is one means of measuring extreme disparities in local incomes. This index is low when high property values and low incomes exist simultaneously in a county and high in the opposite instance; high property values imply the presence of wealth in a county, so simultaneous low average incomes indicate extensive poverty counterbalancing the wealth. Thus, the index moves inversely to income disparities in a county, and E3, based on the index, "rewards" internal equity in income distribution in a county, given a tax rate and mean income.

Efficiency and Compliance with Standards

Efficiency refers to how well a product or service is produced with a given set of resources. The proxy for efficient resource utilization is cost, and were all jails equally "efficient," a jail in low compliance with cost standards would exhibit low operating costs; expenditures would increase with compliance. However, the data suggest that such is not the case and adjustments are necessary to "equalize" jurisdictions for efficiency of operations.

County jails exhibit wide ranges in total costs of operations and average daily costs per inmate (ADC). Such variations may derive from scale considerations, occupancy patterns relative to capacities, and differences in median wages in local labor markets. Simultaneously, the extent to which jails conform to the standards promulgated by the commission varies from locale to locale. Compliance with standards may also imply costs, but not all standards require dollar outlays to assure conformity and not all jails with very high ADCs score high on the compliance scale.

Efficiency is a concern of all governmental units, but the objective of government action is all too often lost in the process of cost minimization. The objectives of examining institutional corrections might be stated in terms of reduced recidivism, lower crime rates, and the like. Alternatively, we note simply that, with reference to impacts on criminality as a whole in society, jails and prisons can be assessed only as components of a justice system that pursue reduced criminality as an objective. In this perspective, the objective may be to get the highest quality of corrections per dollar spent on county jails. Defining "quality" in terms of the jail standards permits the examination of the efficiency with which local facilities conform to the standards.

There are thus two elements to a specification of the efficiency of different correctional institutions: the degree of conformity to standards (the achievement measure C) and the cost of such conformity (the resource use measure R). The optimal installation is the one that maximizes achievement and minimizes resource use, so assuming constant county size, we may express the efficiency measure as a ratio of the achievement measure and the resource use measure. The algebraic terms suggested are:

$$Q = C/R \qquad\qquad (5.1)$$

where Q is an efficiency rating. In real terms, this relation means that two jails having equal average daily costs (for example, an ADC of \$15.00) but different compliance rates (for example 50 percent versus 75 percent) will have, respectively, Q equal to .03 and .05; the latter (.05) indicates more efficient operation or better corrections per dollar. There is thus a logical formula for relating the data elements. The alternative definitions of the measures employed in the construct must be specified, however.

The Achievement Measure

There are 248 standards by which local corrections facilities in Washington have been rated. Of these criteria of quality, some are dollar-cost-free, others imply new operating costs, and yet others require capital outlay, as Table 5-3 indicates. Different combinations of standards and compliance with them may be employed as measures of achievement. Each of these sets of standards can be examined to determine their resource and other implications and to select the most appropriate for use in the reimbursement formula.

Compliance with all standards provides the broadest possible measure of achievement. However, inclusion of the 27 standards requiring potential capital outlays places stress on the capacity of a local jurisdiction to borrow, a condition that may be inappropriate for computation of ongoing subsidies. By contrast, compliance with category A (no-cost) standards only would measure

Table 5-3
Implicit Cost Requirements of Corrections Standards

Requirements		Number of Standards
A. No-cost standards		115
B. Cost standards		133
1. Capital standards	27	
2. Noncapital standards	106	
(a) Increased staffing and/or other increased personnel costs	63	
(b) Increased nonpersonnel operating costs	43	
All standards		248

the effort expended on compliance by institution administration and staff because their rating on these 115 criteria is independent of supplemental cash availability. Although these criteria measure the willingness of personnel to alter their procedures and attitudes towards inmates, it is difficult to provide a rationale for linking these standards to the use of funds. (Unless, of course, reimbursements include a "bonus" for above-average conformance to standards within category A, in which case the ratio measure developed for computations of efficiency is not applicable.)

Compliance to category B-2 (noncapital) standards alone might provide an excellent measure of the extent to which operating funds are employed to increase overall correctional institution quality. This set of standards could be employed either in isolation or combined with category A standards. When used in conjunction with category A standards, the measure of funds utilization is modified by including an indicator of a jurisdiction's willingness to change. This combination appears to be a very useful measure, but the method of combination has serious implications for resulting award patterns. We thus employ three distinct measures of achievement in computing efficiency Q:

1. Achievement measure C1—treats compliance with free (type A) and non-capital cost (type B-2) symmetrically and records total compliance with the 221 standards.
2. Achievement measure C2—trebles the percentage compliance with type-A standards and adds this figure to the percentage compliance with type-B-2 standards. By overweighting compliance with freely attainable standards, this measure places heavier stress on attainment of free standards than does measure C1.
3. Achievement measure C3—totally ignores attainment of type-A standards and permits examination of the cost effectiveness of each jail in using funds to meet standards that have direct budgetary requirements.

The Resource-use Measure

It is important, however, to introduce efficiency of resource usage (as measured through costs) as a modifier of achievement. It was necessary to perform some cost adjustments to make the jails as comparable as possible in light of the difference in median labor costs in urban and rural, affluent and impoverished counties. Regardless of the quality of utilization of resources by a county jail, the institution must pay personnel wages that conform in some measure to the prevailing wage scales in its local labor market. Adjustment of average daily costs per inmate for prevailing wage differences will have a major impact on measured resource use because personnel costs average 76 percent of current operating costs.

The simplest possible adjustment mechanism was the indexed average wage actually paid by jails. The personnel budget for each jail counted as twenty hours per week, or half time. This average cost per man year for personnel was then used to determine a statewide average converted into an index number. The index value, in turn, was used to adjust the recorded personnel cost per inmate day. Two different resource-use measures, the first based on unadjusted wages and the second on adjusted pay, are derived for selected counties in Table 5-4. In the table, $P1$ is the unadjusted personnel cost per inmate day and $P2$ is $P1$ divided by the index wage W for the county. These two personnel-cost measures added to S, the nonpersonnel costs per inmate day yielded two resource-use measures: $R1$, unadjusted or raw costs; and $R2$, adjusted costs.

The Efficiency Rating. It is next necessary to combine achievement with resource usage and derive a numerical index, or indicator. Table 5-5 presents a summary of the various methods of calculating Q, the "efficiency rating" or "quality" indicator.

This net efficiency measure Q, as already noted, is derived through division of the achievement measure by the resource-use measure. Because there are three alternative scales measuring achievement and two measuring resource use, six possible efficiency rating patterns are possible (Appendix G). We have summarized several critical facets of each measure in Appendix G, with the intention that policy makers can select that rating scale that most accurately reflects their perceptions of the appropriate incentives for efficient conformance to standards and disincentives for inefficiency or low-quality jail services.

Reward and reprimand patterns can vary greatly. An appropriate pattern should be selected as the means of promoting efficiency independent of the impact equity considerations will have on the total disbursement pattern. For illustration we will use $Q2$, incorporating $C1$ (compliance with all noncapital standards), and $R2$ (adjusted resource-use measure), as noted above. Once the measure of efficiency has been selected, it can be incorporated with the equity formula and the basic disbursement scheme described. This scheme requires modification to maximize its effectiveness or impact in producing desired outcomes. Such modifications are the subject of the next section.

Table 5-4

Costs, Wage Differentials, and Resource Use by Jails, Selected Washington Counties

County	Index Wage (W)	Personnel Costs Per Inmate Day Raw (P_1)	Adjusted $(P_2 = P_1/W)$	Other Current Costs Per Inmate Day (S)	Total Inmate Raw $(R_1 = P_1 + S)$	Costs Per Day Adjusted $(R_2 = P_2 + S)$
A	1.6369	11.29	6.90	2.79	14.08	9.69
B	0.9448	12.23	12.94	4.24	16.47	17.18
C	1.0330	4.13	3.99	1.42	5.55	5.41
D	0.8378	4.69	5.59	1.95	6.64	7.54
E	1.0089	6.24	6.18	0.77	7.01	6.95
F	1.2402	16.54	13.33	2.61	19.15	15.94
G	0.8761	5.19	5.92	1.68	6.87	7.60
H	1.0298	6.86	6.66	4.08	10.94	10.74
J	1.2329	10.96	8.89	8.65	19.61	17.54
K	0.7593	5.06	6.66	2.33	7.39	8.99
Averages					13.80	13.97

Table 5-5

Alternative Efficiency Rating Scales, Selected Washington Counties

County	$Q_1 = C_1/R_1$	$Q_2 = C_1/R_2$	$Q_3 = C_2/R_1$	$Q_4 = C_2/R_2$	$Q_5 = C_3/R_1$	$Q_6 = C_3/R_2$
A	10.53	15.32	21.18	30.80	5.21	7.58
B	11.17	10.71	22.82	21.88	5.34	5.12
C	31.35	32.16	64.14	65.80	15.95	15.34
D	20.63	18.16	44.57	39.25	9.78	8.62
E	17.58	17.22	35.35	34.62	8.69	8.76
F	9.45	11.17	19.37	22.90	4.49	5.30
G	24.01	21.71	49.92	45.13	11.06	10.00
H	16.45	16.75	33.82	34.45	7.76	7.91
J	7.70	8.61	15.75	17.61	3.67	4.10
K	17.58	14.45	36.07	29.65	8.34	6.85

The Overall Efficiency Rating. The achievement scales and the resource-use measures may now be combined in accordance with the formula displayed in Equation (5.1) to arrive at the overall efficiency rating. Table 5-5 displays the value of the efficiency rating for the six possible Q scales (based on two R scales and three C scales) for selected counties in Washington. Examination of this table indicates that not only do the relative magnitudes of the rating applied to counties shift considerably from one scale to another, but the rank order in which the counties would be placed according to a scale also changes from one Q measure to another. Detailed examination of the characteristics of each of the rating measures, therefore, would be required for policy makers to make a choice among the six available alternatives.

Disregarding the issue of the ordering of the counties, we may base one dimension of the choice of Q measures to employ on the distributional impact of the different scales, indicated in Table 5-6. The difference in the ratio of high value to low value for the six different Q scales is significant, with $Q6$ showing the starkest disparity and $Q4$ the slightest. Examination of the percentage allocation shares, however, suggests that the real impact in terms of differences in payments would be starkest in $Q1$, which shows the greatest difference in pay-outs to the top jurisdiction and the low jurisdiction and between pay-outs to the top five jurisdictions and the low five local areas. The policy decision about how to reward efficiency would therefore have to be based on more than just apparent distributional impact and would have to return to the logic underlying the derivation of the Q scales, that is, to the R and C measures themselves.

Table 5-6
Distributional Characteristics of Efficiency Scales[a]

Range of Indexed Values	Q_1	Q_2	Q_3	Q_4	Q_5	Q_6
High value	3.13	2.66	2.98	2.52	3.00	2.67
Mean value	1.00	1.00	1.00	1.00	1.00	1.00
Low value	0.17	0.15	0.16	0.15	0.16	0.11
(High value)/(low value)	18.41	17.73	18.62	16.80	18.75	24.27
Percentage Allocation Shares						
Top jurisdiction	7.01%	6.06%	6.78%	5.72%	6.82%	6.04%
Top 5 jurisdictions	25.44	24.92	25.45	24.55	25.35	24.40
Mean jurisdiction	2.24	2.27	2.28	2.27	2.27	2.26
Low 5 jurisdictions	2.39	2.35	2.67	2.65	2.40	2.28
Low jurisdiction	0.38	0.35	0.37	0.34	0.36	0.26
Top minus low	6.63	5.71	6.41	5.38	6.46	5.78
Top 5 minus low 5	23.05	22.57	22.78	21.90	22.95	22.12

[a]All scales normalized to show mean value of 1.00.

Efficacy in Subsidies: Assuring Impact on County Corrections

Subsidies, as indicated above, constitute a total or partial assumption of the costs of production of an output by an agency other than the provider in order to enable the provider to in some measure upgrade the total production (either by increasing the volume of output or by upgrading its quality). The magnitude of the subsidy reflects decisions about the payments necessary to assure that the subsidy accomplishes its purpose. Overpayment constitutes a waste of financial resources if a lower payment would have produced the desired outcomes.

Efficacy criteria, therefore, are not formulas based on abstract principles or standards, but rather constitute judgments about the "best" uses of available subsidy funds. In other words, efficacy, or impact on actions taken with respect to matters deemed important by the grantor, is really a statewide efficiency measure. The allocation formula adopted, subject to some constraints from the political arena, should be the one that will increase the statewide conformance to the standards for local jails as much as is possible within a given budgetary limitation. The form that such efficacy criteria most typically will take, therefore, is that of a constraint on allowable subsidy levels and grants to small localities.

The largest county in Washington State, for example, contains one-third of all the state's residents. If a straight per-capital allocation of subsidies for local jails were employed, it follows that this jurisdiction would get one-third of the funds allocated for the subsidy program. However, this county simultaneously has far higher quality jails than do the majority of other counties in the state, and dilution of the dollar subsidy pool for which the other counties could compete by one-third, simply on a principle of equal distribution, would undermine the ability of the subsidy program to attain its supposed ends: a statewide improvement in local jails.

By contrast, the smallest counties in the state, which contained as few as 3800 people in 1974, may be extremely inefficient units in which to attempt to provide jail services. One standard, for example, requires that a facility be staffed twenty-four hours a day, seven days a week. This provision would produce astronomical average daily costs for a small jail with an average population of one or two inmates. Provision of any subsidy at all to such small units may be counterproductive in terms of efficient utilization of the funds to increase the overall quality of local jails. Denial of any subsidy to units which are so small as to be inevitably highly inefficient may produce incentives for multiple county jointures within which a single jail could be maintained at lower costs to the counties *and* the state.

The process of utilization for such efficacy criteria is best explained by way of illustration. For this purpose, we adopt the following measures from the efficiency and equity ratings derived below. The measures are not employed here because they are superior to the other rating scales—a judgment of superiority is a political decision that lies within the province of the appropriate decision makers—but simply in order to permit the presentation of a well-rounded example.

We will utilize the overall efficiency rating, the $Q2$ value for a county. This is the achievement measure taken across all the corrections standards not requiring capital outlays, weighting zero cost and positive cost standards equally, divided by the resource use adjusted for wage differentials. In addition, we will make use of an equity-efficiency rating combining the E and Q measures in an aggregated scale. For this combined rating, we derive $D*$ according to the following formula:

$$D* = E3(C1/R2) = (E3)(Q2) \qquad (5.2)$$

Thus, the equity scale derived from the income extraction capability index has been used in conjunction with the straightforward $Q2$ scale to arrive at a joint rating scale.

The overall efficiency rating $Q2$ can be employed to define criteria for a floor on subsidy payments. The ability of a jurisdiction to utilize revenues is the essential consideration in cutting off subsidy funds. For jurisdictions with efficiency ratings that are below some defined percentage of the state mean efficiency, no subsidy should be provided. Denial of funds would produce a stimulus to combine jails and consolidate across county lines and, in turn, through increased scale, would produce higher efficiency levels and result in state subsidy payments to the new, combined facilities. This initial subsidy denial might produce greater long-run efficacy in the subsidy program. The minimum acceptable efficiency level may be derived from data on the costs of attaining desired levels of output quality. With reference to maximum or ceiling disbursements, we look at $D*$, the equity-efficiency rating for all counties. If that rating, for any one county, exceeds some multiple of the average rating, then the county should be limited to the ceiling cut-off level. This proposed maximum derives from a concern with the return of subsidy dollars and recognition that any tendency towards overpayment for one county implies a concomitant tendency towards underfunding of other counties.

Before we turn to an examination of the distributional characteristics of $D*$ and of a comparable measure incorporating floors and ceilings on per-capita subsidy payments, we should note that efficacy requirements include demonstration of continuing performance in response to subsidy grants over time. Given a constant dollar pool and improving average institutional quality, any facility that does not improve should find its reimbursement falling over time. This provision is appropriate for the maximization of efficacy. However, the incentives to upgrade may be strengthened by a requirement that, in order to be eligible for funds in excess of those granted in the base year of the program, a county must either be in 100 percent conformance to standards (excluding capital construction based standards) or show an improvement in conformance amounting to at least some specified proportion of the percentages nonconformance. (Thus, assuming a one-fifth proportion for illustrative purposes, a county in 80 percent compliance would have to raise its compliance level to 84 percent, but a county in 50 percent compliance would have to climb to 60 percent compliance to get increased funds.)

In summary, efficacy considerations require that the equity and efficiency bases for allocation of subsidy funds be augmented by maximum and minimum levels of allowed grants per capita to counties if the subsidy program itself is to operate at the highest possible level of efficacy. Incentives for gradual upgrading of the degree of conformance to standards should also be developed if the subsidy program is to do more than maintain a given level of jail quality or provide a one-shot upgrading of jails.

Conclusion: Interaction Effects and Budget Constraints

Detailing all the interaction effects and related patterns of imposition of efficacy adjustments of per-capita allocations associated with an efficiency-equity rating is a monumental task. Given three different E (equity) measures and six Q (efficiency) scales, there exist eighteen possible efficiency-equity ratings. Each would require at least one efficacy adjustment and preferably more than that. Thus, this concluding discussion can but illustrate the possible interaction effects and the implication of overplaying efficacy constraints on subsidy patterns dictated by equity and efficiency alone.

The example that will be employed was alluded to above, with an equity-efficiency index D^* derived by Equation (5.2) from $E3$ and $Q2$. The efficacy adjustment that will be employed is as follows:

1. No jurisdiction shall receive a per-capita subsidy in excess of 150 percent of the state mean level, as recommended based on D^*.
2. No jurisdiction that does not exhibit an efficiency rating of at least 35 percent of the state mean $Q2$ rating will be eligible for any subsidy funding.

The adjustment has the effect of reducing the per-capita subsidy available to four counties in the state with a very high D^* and eliminating the subsidy altogether for five counties with very low $Q2$ scores.

The distributional characteristics for local jurisdictions under the assumption of equal populations of the D^* measures and the adjusted measure S^* are presented in Table 5-7. The S^* column is split in half for presentation of data on the "low" jurisdictions, because this label can be applied either to the five counties denied a subsidy under the adjustment or to the next lowest counties, the bottom five counties having been removed altogether. The impact of removal

Table 5-7
Distributional Characteristics of Efficiency-Equity Scales

Range of Indexed Values	D*	S*	
High value	3.08	1.50	
Mean value	1.00	1.00	
Low value	0.12	0.44[a]	0.00[b]
(High value)/(low value)	25.67	3.41	
Percentage Allocation Shares			
Top jurisdiction	9.00	4.40	4.40
Top 5 jurisdictions	24.40	21.10	21.10
Mean jurisdiction	2.90	3.20	3.20
Low 5 jurisdictions	3.60	8.30	0.00
Low jurisdiction	0.40	1.50	0.00
Top minus low	8.60	2.90	4.40
Top 5 minus low 5	20.80	12.80	21.10

[a]Deleting the five jurisdictions denied a subsidy in the computations.
[b]Retaining the five jurisdictions denied a subsidy in the computations.

of the five extremely weak counties from the total sample is not insignificant. The S* computations assume that the total subsidy available remains unchanged from that attainable under the D* formula. Thus, the share of the total going to the highest jurisdictions falls due to the ceiling provision, whereas the pool available for all counties other than the five denied any subsidy increases by the amount of money that would have gone to the units that scored very low on the efficiency-equity scale.

First, note that the share of the top counties, whether measured in ratio terms relative to the mean or low counties or in terms of percentage allocations, falls significantly due to the ceiling. Given limited funds, it is perhaps appropriate to be cautious about devoting an excessive percentage of the total to any one jurisdiction. Simultaneously, the redistribution away from the top jurisdictions that were above the ineligibility cutoff appeared as the new "low" five jurisdictions under S*. Under the D* allocations, these jurisdictions would have received only 7.2 percent of the disbursements, so their share rises by 14 percent to 8.3 percent in the adjusted scale for distribution. Finally, the other jurisdictions—falling between the top five and the bottom five—also benefit in terms of additional shares of the total pool of funds, as indicated in the rise of the share of the "mean" jurisdiction from 2.9 to 3.2, a 10 percent increase.

To summarize the discussion of subsidy formulas, we must now return to the issue of the actual populations in different counties. All of the comparisons conducted thus far in the discussion of allocational shares have assumed that the population in each county was the same. Obviously, this assumption is invalid; the largest county in Washington contains one-third of the total population of the state. The allocation shares accruing to this large county will thus be a major proportion of the total subsidy payments, simply by virtue of the magnitude of its population. It follows, however, that if this county and other counties with above average total populations have above average ratings on the D^* efficiency-equity scale, the imposition of a ceiling on the magnitude of per-capita grants relative to the mean would distribute a far greater proportion of funds to smaller counties than would be the case if all counties had equal population.

Because the economies of scale associated with jail operations tend to cause the larger jurisdictions' facilities to have lower than average resource-use levels (R scales), the efficiency or Q scale tends to be greater for the major counties. The high Q score of course, translates into a higher than average D^* rating in the absence of massive intercounty differences in incomes and property valuations (which did not appear to be present). Thus, the imposition of a ceiling on per-capita subsidies would tend to take large amounts of money away from the major counties and redistribute it towards the smaller jurisdictions. With reference to the five top jurisdictions in Table 5-7, for example, the share of total state population living in those jurisdictions was 48 percent. Any reduction in the subsidy to one-half the state's population, of course, would provide roughly equal increases in the subsidy going to other jurisdictions. The result of the interaction between D^* and S^* and the county populations is demonstrated for selected counties in Table 5-8.

Table 5-8
Shares of Total Subsidy to Local Jails

County	Percent Share of Total Subsidy Under	
	D^* Allocation	S^* Allocation
A	41.6%	36.1%
B	1.4	1.6
C	12.3	9.3
D	3.4	3.9
E	1.2	1.4
F	0.06	0.07
G	4.1	4.8
H	0.26	0.30
J	0.12	0.00
K	0.16	0.18
All counties	100%	100%

Counties A and C, among those selected, clearly would have their total shares reduced by a ceiling on the magnitude of any per-capita subsidy. The other counties therefore would increase their shares of the total subsidy. One exception was present in the selected set, however: County J ranked so low on the efficiency measure $Q2$ that it was denied any subsidy under the efficacy-adjusted formula of S^*. The efficacy adjustment, then interacts with the efficiency-equity rating schedule to increase the impact of the subsidy dollars employed by the state in recognition of the need to consider a locality's ability to utilize large grants (which accounts for the imposition of a ceiling) and the need to avoid granting subsidies to jurisdictions that would under no conditions be in a position to successfully and efficiently provide high-quality local jail services.

Equity adjustments, by themselves, provide no stimulus to specific action, so such a basis would be inadequate for a subsidy designed to encourage a particular activity of local government. Efficiency alone, however, fails to recognize the inequities imposed on some localities by particular economic circumstances and population patterns and would provide funds where they would not be absorbable or to localities that could not become efficient in service delivery. The combination of the two measures would correct for inequities but still could not assure that funds provided in subsidies would be efficiently utilized. The efficient utilization of subsidy monies, that is, the efficacious allocation of state funds to local jurisdictions to achieve a state's purpose, must therefore incorporate a specific set of adjustments reflecting current priorities and political considerations, along with any allocational formula. The formula provides a base for the subsidy allocation decision, but the final distribution pattern should incorporate constraints derived from the politics of the decision-making environment. In the case of the state of Washington, these constraints should be such as to contribute to the state's goals of stronger local capacities for incarceration.

Capital Cost Considerations

Regardless of the final pattern of ongoing subsidies for jail operations, a separate issue presents itself with respect to the sharing of capital construction costs between the state and local jurisdictions. Capital costs and conformance to the standards that may require capital outlays differ from the costs and standards for other aspects of jails in several critical regards:

1. Capital outlays occur at a point in time, unlike operating costs, which must be provided for over time.
2. Gradual adjustments in budgets, such as are possible in the incremental upgrading of jail staff and other operations elements, are not feasible with

respect to capital improvements, a large number of which are indivisible, that is, all-or-nothing decisions.

3. Conformance to commission standards relating to the physical condition of jails may be unattainable without capital outlays, so no amount of "goodwill" in the absence of funds could improve the conformance rating of a facility.

4. Execution of a plan of capital improvements may automatically produce conformance with a large number of standards in the absence of effort beyond the expenditure of funds for construction.

For all these reasons, then, because standards compliance may be rigidly associated with capital expenditures and the volume of such expenditures may be an indivisible burden falling on a jurisdiction at a specific point in time, the capital cost problem is significantly different from that associated with other spending.

The discussion below is based on the assumption that the Law Enforcement Assistance Administration's 50 percent formula for federal shares in state prison construction can be extended downward to state-local sharing. Unlike the federal government, however, some states (and Washington is one) may wish to exercise discretion in the allocation of state monies for local-jail capital improvements. Obviously, the 50 percent formula could be applied to all jurisdictions, on the basis that the state is willing to pay for upgrading of corrections facilities in counties, and all outlays for construction would convert directly into closer conformance to the standards for local jails.

This approach, however, denies the presence of interactions between the quality of the physical condition of a jail and the pattern of effort directed at meeting nonphysically based jail standards. There is reason to believe that an improved physical setting improves the attitude of staff and might increase conformance to those standards that have been identified as essentially costless. Moreover, the provision of physical facilities in the absence of staff that permit the jail residents access to the facilities would not increase the compliance of a local jail with all recommended standards. Finally, a facility may be upgraded physically for a client population that is so small that it is inefficient to maintain the jail in the first place. For these reasons, some adjustment in the state formula is in order, although the mean state share may well remain 50 percent.

These problem areas, of course, have just been addressed. Inclusion of the ceiling on per-capita subsidies and the floor on the productivity and efficiency required for the grant of any subsidy—that is, the efficacy considerations—along with the general efficiency and equity measures produces an index of "worthiness" that is as applicable to the sharing of construction costs as it is to provision of continuing subsidies. Because the objective of a capital construction cost sharing formula, however, is that one-half, or 50 percent, of all jail construction in the state be paid for by the state government, a specially indexed version of the allocational formula designated S^* must be constructed for capital cost sharing.

The construction of a formula for computation of the state's share of capital construction costs in any county is straightforward. A series of variables needs to be defined, however. Let us therefore take

NEWCONS	= total value of all state-authorized new construction for local jails (where state authorization excludes construction in jurisdictions denied subsidies under the S^* formula)
NEWCONS(i)	= total value of new construction in County "i"
SINDEX(i)	= the S^* value for County "i" indexed to the state mean S^* value, such that the new mean is 1.00
WGTCONS(i)	= (NEWCONS(i))(SINDEX(i)) = the weighted value of the authorized new construction in County "i"
WGTCONS	= total value of all weighted construction costs across all counties (the sum of all the WGTCONS(i), across i)
RATIO	= WGTCONS/NEWCONS = the ratio of the weighted to the unweighted statewide value of all authorized new construction
SHARE1(i)	= authorized state share (percent of total) of construction in County "i" under formula (5.3) below
SHARE2(i)	= authorized state share (percent of total) of construction in County "i" under formula (5.4) below.

We can now turn to the specification of the formulas themselves.

Formula (5.3) is very straightforward: it simply takes the indexed subsidy to a county and uses it to determine the state share of construction costs by applying the 50 percent adjustment to the subsidy measure:

$$SHARE1(i) = (0.5)(SINDEX(i)) \qquad (5.3)$$

Under this formulation, because the indexed S^* cannot exceed 1.50, the state's share of construction cannot exceed 75 percent. Under this construct however, the state's share of the total construction may deviate from 50 percent because the construction, when weighted by SINDEX(i), may total a different dollar amount than the unweighted total. There is no assurance that WGTCONS will equal NEWCONS, and only if the two are equal will the state's share of the total authorized statewide construction be precisely 50 percent.

Formula (5.4) utilizes the unweighted and weighted total state construction costs to adjust the shares for each county's construction in order to assure that the statewide average is precisely 50 percent:

$$\text{SHARE2(i)} = \text{(RATIO)(SHARE1(i))} = \text{(0.5)(SINDEX(i))(RATIO)} \quad (5.4)$$

There is no particular preference for either of these two formulas. Both derive from the logic, already explicated in detail, of the state subsidy schedule. The second formulation may be preferable to the first in that it assures the state that, for an anticipated total construction cost, the state's share would be precisely one-half the total. The first formulation cannot predict the total dollar value of the state's construction contribution with comparable assurance.

Knowing what subsidy schedule reflects state planning and political priorities, a policy maker can translate the subsidy formula into a mechanism for sharing construction and other capital costs. Note that the 50 percent total share accepted by the state is not a given and another share level may be employed. Whatever share value actually is chosen may replace the 0.50 figure in Equations (5.3) and (5.4).

Note

1. R.L. Smith, "A Quiet Revolution: Probation Subsidy," *Delinquency Prevention Reporter* (May 1971), pp. 3-7.

6 Conclusions

The current condition and future prospects for the local jail can be understood only in light of the institution's historical development, unique characteristics, and position in the nation's criminal justice system. Standing at the crossroads between sometimes conflicting interests, the jail, its keepers, and its kept have been subjected to forces beyond their purview and sphere of influence.

Humanitarian concern in the late eighteenth and early nineteenth century gave impetus to legal reforms that substantially reduced the number of offenses punishable by mutilation, hanging, and other extreme measures. The result, however, was the creation of state-operated institutions for major offenders who earlier would have been dealt with summarily. In its new prisons, America changed the "workhouse" concept of seventeenth-century Europe by including long-term sentences; thus, jails were left with the less serious, sentenced offenders and those detained awaiting trial—at a time when there were reportedly more than enough beds in the local counties' jails. Why the state assumed the function is lost in historical obscurity. There was a precedent for jailing debtors, drunks, prostitutes, and other minor violators, whereas difficult cases were treated with means not requiring incarceration. Whatever the reasons, less drastic penalties coupled with the penitence and work-oriented philosophy in penology produced a local institution that has resisted basic change until the present.

On any given day, there are between 140,000 and 150,000 persons confined in jails throughout the United States. Yet the figures tell only part of the story, because many more are committed and released annually. The ratio of average daily population to total commitments has been estimated to vary widely between 1:34 and 1:11. This high turnover places special strains on intake processes and makes personalized treatment a pipe dream. Jail staff have little time for anything more than booking, shakedown, cell assignment, dress out, booking, shakedown. . . .

The turnover might be manageable if the clients—sentenced and detainees—were more homogeneous. However, prisoners include ordinance violators, all types of misdemeanants, and felons of varying degree. Those serving sentences—short and long—commingle with detainees awaiting trial, sentencing, or transfer. Sophisticated criminals come in contact with the first-time offender. The relative population mix of a jail affects its primary mission, thereby contributing to its uniqueness. Frequently, conflicting objectives (say, detention versus rehabilitation) contribute to unmanageability.

To these complexities is added the combination of jail operations with law enforcement functions, which by themselves are already difficult and multi-faceted. Historical happenstance, more than political, economic, or management logic, has placed responsibility at the local level in the hands of elected officials. As a consequence, approximately three out of every four jails accommodate twenty or fewer prisoners; it is questionable whether on this scale jails can ever operate efficiently, either from a monetary or social point of view.

In some respects, the above generalizations obscure national diversity. New York and Chicago have large, urban jails that exceed the capacities of many state institutions. North Carolina houses sentenced misdemeanants serving over thirty days in state camps.

Washington State recognized the need to address these local jail problems as early as 1962 and ten years later the policy decision was made (as it was in many states) that standards were the way to improve conditions. The unique feature of Washington's decision, however, was the statutory requirement to estimate implementation costs before promulgating standards. In some respects, the cost estimates for proposed standards reported in earlier chapters were staggering: $46 million—almost 600 percent more than 1974 operating costs for all jails—is probably beyond the reach of any state in the short run. Even if the costs were fundable over a five-to-ten-year period, the basic assumptions that produced the standards that created the cost remain unexamined.

Standards

In the course of any study, there are always questions, observations and thoughts that, however interesting and important, are beyond the available time, resources, or stated objectives. While enmeshed in the details of the estimation process, the authors found themselves becoming increasingly interested in some of the conceptual issues and assumptions underlying standards development in the public sector, intergovernmental relations and responsibilities, and possible effects of jail standards on other elements of the criminal justice system or on the broader social services field.

Standards have become the principal social policy tool for improving local jails, but it is not clear why. It may be that the American tradition of local control combined with the political nature of jail management require an administrative arrangement that diffuses responsibility and centralizes authority, but allows participation by varying interests. There is not, however, a self-evident, state interest that fully explains its involvement. The pretrial-detention function is a service to the judiciary and, therefore, may be of interest to a unified court system. To a limited degree, jails may be a safety valve for overcrowded state institutions. State officials simply may now have a broader perspective of the criminal justice system as a result of federal requirements to create comprehensive plans in return for subsidies. Nevertheless, these reasons do not seem persuasive in the face of potential legal, economic, and political pitfalls assumed by state involvement. By choosing to intercede, the state opens itself to liabilities that are not trivial with an active judiciary. As shown in Washington, the price of securing county and city concurrence with standards is likely to be more demands on an already depleted treasury. It is naive to believe state financing will not require some measure of state control (if for no other reason than fiduciary responsibility), but this prospect simply adds to the political complexities already inherent in state-local relations.

Confronted with conditions that offend all except the most calloused observer, professionals, elected officials, and citizen reform groups have turned (almost in desperation) to standards as the catalyst for a more decent jail. Why? As a measure of performance and a criterion of excellence, a set of standards raises many unanswered policy questions:

1. How should standards be formulated? How are the social policy objectives they are designed to achieve articulated?
2. Have they been "effective" in accomplishing their purpose(s) with these social institutions?
3. When are standards so general as to be meaningless or too specific to be equitably applied?
4. Have standards affected the nature of intergovernmental relations?
5. Is money alone a sufficient incentive for assuring compliance with standards? Do subsidies from higher levels of government affect the distribution of costs and benefits? Who pays and who gathers the returns?
6. What management tools are needed to implement standards? What acceptable enforcement mechanisms are available (for example, facility or staff accreditation) and effective?

Establishing and implementing standards in an area as complicated as jail operations and management represent a major undertaking in any jurisdiction. Added to this is the difficulty of attempting to evaluate the interaction effects within the criminal justice system, the validity of different cost analyses, the benefits derived from upgrading jails, and who should pay.

Priorities and Resources

In a market economy, individuals and firms face choices about how to allocate scarce resources among alternative wants. Scarcity is not confined to private decisions, however, and public bodies are increasingly obliged to address the problem of financial constraints, which involves prioritizing needs.

Chapter 2 discussed the need to structure a set of standards in such a way that their response implications can be estimated and so decision makers have a frame of reference for choosing priorities subject to resource constraints. Estimating economic impact would be greatly facilitated if this framework were established simultaneously with standards themselves. Perhaps just as important, this tie with fiscal realities would reduce the vagueness endemic to most standards setting and require clearer statements of the goals and objectives that the policies are designed to achieve.

The structure used in Chapter 3 was tailored to the specific needs of Washington State officials: capital and noncapital standards were distinguished; the latter were partitioned into those requiring staff for implementation; and high-compliance standards were separated from low-compliance standards. What was lacking, however, because it must be resolved through the political process, was a precise statement of policy direction. The commission's proposed legislation to codify the results says the intent is to provide "a humane and safe environment consistent with efficient use of funds." Although an admirable statement of social philosophy, it does not lend itself to operationalization. This shortcoming is evident from the fact that a standard requiring staff of the same sex as prisoners produces a relatively high cost for small jails. It is not that the standard is unnecessary, only that implementing it is probably inconsistent with efficient use of funds. So the absence of a policy statement regarding regionalization or consolidation creates a dilemma: either compliance requirements must be relaxed for small jails, funds allocated to inefficient operations, or incentives structured to create more efficient jails. The lack of policy objectives, inherent vagueness, and an absence of structure to assist in choosing priorities make it more difficult to answer the inevitable question of resource needs and to decide on specific resource allocations.

Subsidies

Jail problems historically are as much a result of shortcomings in the entire constellation of criminal justice and social service agencies as the result of political disinterest or official misfeasance. Trial delays, prosecutorial discretion, criminalizing health problems, ignoring the poor, and similar realities share the blame. Yet, the pleas of the systems analyst and professional planner for a more orderly approach to solutions will probably remain unheeded in the interest of political and pragmatic expediency. Subsidies, like other solutions in isolation, are appealing because they appear to reduce the local financial burden of standards compliance and make state-imposed regulations more acceptable to the electorate. The jail is subject—more so than other criminal justice agencies— to executive, legislative, and judicial forces beyond its direct control. Police practices and prosecutors' decisions impact directly and immediately and create the potential for wide fluctuations in population. The impact of new criminal laws is felt first at the jail before there is an opportunity to reduce downstream effects by diversion, by fines, by probation. Jails sit in the mainstream, subject to the vagaries of public opinion, court scheduling, prosecutorial discretion, legislative initiatives, and prison capacity.

Any subsidy to only one component of an interdependent system such as criminal justice may create negative effects, so extreme care should be exercised in designing subsidy systems. For example, a jail subsidy by itself is an incentive for local officials to choose this alternative rather than summonses or diversion, because it reduces the relative cost of incarceration to the jurisdiction. Payments geared to a facility's average daily population are an economic incentive to increase incarceration rates. This force becomes stronger as the per-capita payments become greater than the marginal cost of incarceration over some range of population. If the daily cost of adding five persons is, say, $3.00 each for food, clothing, and processing and the subsidy is $5.00 per prisoner day, local jurisdictions can realize a net revenue gain by increasing their average daily jail population. This effect could be countered by reducing payments as populations rise above some base-period norm. If the policy objective is to reduce proportionately the number of persons incarcerated at the state level, then the ratio of state to local prisoners (either statewide or on a county-by-county basis) can be introduced into the subsidy formula. Reducing the period of pretrial incarceration can be encouraged by reducing the per-capita subsidy by some amount for each day, week, or month beyond a specified date after incarceration.

These few examples belie the complexities, because they do not focus on specific, desired results internal to the jails and they ignore the quality of services delivered. Attempts to introduce these considerations have typically involved imposing some form of standard (with or without cash subsidies), but it may be possible to produce the same results more simply by means of noncash subsidies. Many aspects of jails operations could be improved by having the state deliver services directly and, thereby, indirectly subsidize local governments. Quality control and standards then would be under direct state control with a local option to participate. For example, mobile classrooms operated by state employees could visit jails regularly to conduct academic or other classes for sentenced prisoners free of charge. State-employed, drug-treatment counselors could similarly circulate between jurisdictions supervising group sessions or linking releasees to available community resources. In the management area, developing a local information-system capability may be a particularly appropriate program for noncash subsidization. The state could provide systems design services and make data processing available without charge. Systems could vary in sophistication and be designed to fit the unique needs of each jail, but at the same time they would be compatible in certain basic features. Small jails, for example, may have a need only for identification, age, sex, offense, and similar data that are routinely collected during the booking process. Medium-sized facilities could add court disposition information, and large jails could include information on family status, occupation and work history, prior criminal record, test scores, and program participation.

The above suggestions assume no universally applicable standards, but it is possible to introduce noncash subsidies once standards have been developed. In this case, the locality still has the option of refusing the subsidy, but it then must provide the services itself. This scheme allows the state to establish priority areas within the broad and several mandates of standards implementation and may be particularly relevant where state funds are constrained and jail improvement must take place over time. For example, during the first funding cycle, medical care—whether in the form of a "circuit-riding" doctor or a mobile mini-hospital—may be the only subsidized activity and the only area for which localities are responsible for standards compliance. In succeeding years, services could be added in some order of importance based on statewide needs and resources.

Noncash subsidies may be a politically more acceptable way of imposing standards considered desirable by the state, preserving some degree of local option, retaining fiscal accountability nearer the funding source and assuring performance through direct control.

Future Research

Despite the fact that jail problems have plagued officials for centuries, research on jails is abysmally scanty when compared to corrections, mental institutions, hospitals, and the like. Even baseline, descriptive statistics have been available only for a few years, and these figures have their limitations. Therefore, it seems more than appropriate to exercise the "noblesse oblige" of the social scientist to end every book, article, and research report with a plea for future inquiry. Spawned as much by simple curiosity as they are by economic self-interest, these entreaties sometimes indiscriminately call for everything at once without regard to social policy needs or available resources.

The number of jails, their diversity, and the complexity of the issues almost overwhelm anyone who considers jail research; even relatively modest efforts, if comprehensive, will consume substantial resources. In addition to the inherent complexities and resource constraints, however, it seems logically appropriate first to attempt a better *description* of the political, administrative, social, and economic dimensions of the jail phenomenon. Unconstitutional and degrading conditions will not permit decision makers to await the scientist's final judgment, but more systematically derived knowledge about local jails is necessary before plans for improvement can be chosen with any reasonable prospect for success. One of the frustrations of past research has been the nonexistence of mechanisms for translating findings into action. Clues or hypotheses about *why* things are as they are should flow from a thorough description of *how* they are today. This does not preclude, of course, carefully targeted interim demonstration projects, but these projects should be undertaken with an eye toward multiple dimensions, systemic effects, and generalizability. A health care project in a specific jail, for example, offers few benefits to other county jails unless it addresses the general problem of health care in rural locales, incorporates a strategy for local assumption, considers the effects of the jail's internal environment, and seeks alternatives to incarceration for alcoholics and drug abusers. This is not to say that a $50 or even a $500,000 project must take on the cares of the world; it means only that a one-time, isolated effort must be aware of and strive for longer-term, widespread effects.

Knowledge rather than parochialism further constrains the authors to limit recommendations to *economic* research. These constraints are not trivial, given the financial condition of most city, county, and state governments, and even the federal government; but the need for economic research should be evaluated in relation to needs for a better understanding of the political forces hampering jail reform, the managerial problems resulting from changing populations and untrained staff, effects on families and employment of even short-term detention, and a host of other unanswered questions.

The Social Cost of Jails

Virtually nothing is known about what economists call the "opportunity cost" of various practices typically carried out by jails. What opportunities are forgone by deciding to hold persons awaiting trial or removing people from the labor market to serve thirty-day sentences? If jail improvement is to proceed from a comprehensive base that includes interaction effects, it is necessary to estimate the economic cost of current practices in order to compare them to alternative approaches. A diversion program may appear costly in isolation, but if it results in renewed or continued employment, the long-run cost to the community may be less than the cost of recurring periods of short-term incarceration. Even after accounting for increased risk, issuing summons in lieu of arrest and detention may be a more cost-effective way of assuring appearance at trial by allowing the principal breadwinner to remain on the job.

More directly, jails seldom report accurately their direct costs. Utilities charges frequently appear in a courthouse budget, fringe benefits are financed from a county's general fund, charges for the physical plant are hidden in construction accounts, and law enforcement functions performed by jail employees confound true detention costs. Services may be supplied directly by the county health department but never charged to the cost of incarceration.

Managers and elected officials need and taxpayers deserve complete cost information if they are to make rational economic choices. Although the formal proof is too complicated to present here, understating production costs in a market environment results in a suboptimal allocation of resources among alternative outputs; that is, less is forthcoming in the aggregate because too much of one and too little of another product or service are produced. Therefore, if the social cost of jails is understated and the decision maker must choose between detention and diversion, the incarceration rate would be higher than it would if all costs were considered. The choice may be made for noneconomic reasons, as well, but one should at least know what is being forgone—the "price," say, of a safer community.

Allocating Direct Costs

Because the jail is a potpourri of law enforcement, judicial, rehabilitation, and social functions, the direct and indirect monetary costs (even if accurately computed) have not been allocated to these various activities so that programmatic choices internal to the jail can be made. Assuming the opportunity costs of alternatives are known, there is a second set of decisions regarding the most efficient "production" process, given existing techniques and practices.

Chapter 3 presented an initial (albeit too simplistic) structuring of 248 standards around 18 functions performed by jails. With a more refined and better defined structure, this approach would provide a basis for estimating the cost of specific jail activities (for example, intake processing, surveillance, and court appearances) and for isolating factors (such as turnover) that determine fixed and variable costs in both the short and long run. Only with this information can managers begin to evaluate alternative techniques, methods, and practices with objective criteria. Closed-circuit television, for example, may not be desirable for philosophical reasons, but if it permits staff reallocation to functions deemed more important than surveillance, it may be an acceptable alternative for economic reasons. In addition, resource allocations do reflect priorities (at least implicitly), but cost information categorized in terms of functions, activities, and ultimately organizational objectives makes these priorities explicit and open to examination.

Optimum Scale of Plant

Better estimates of economic cost and a more precise specification of the functions comprising a jail's "production process" would significantly improve the prospects for answering the recurring question "What size jail?" To date, this question has been treated as an architectural one with some crumbs thrown to the social psychologist, but there are also fundamental economic aspects that must accompany the search for a solution. Regionalization and consolidation issues can never be resolved objectively (except where gross diseconomies exist) without knowing how many beds and, hence, the size of the area to be covered. The studies by Block and Mikesell reported at the end of Chapter 1 imaginatively drew upon various indicators of quantity (for example, man-days of incarceration) and quality (for example, square feet per inmate and prisoner death rates), but each was limited due either to incomplete cost data such as capital or to the inability to measure "output" based on published sources.

Effects of Subsidies

Finally, there has not been economic research on the effects of criminal justice subsidies (with the exception of probation subsidy). Before corrections—or any criminal justice field for that matter—begins careening down the road to another treasury, subsidies should be examined empirically. Are they equitable? Efficient? Effective? Or more basically, what action are we attempting to elicit? Should subsidies be tied to performance? The criminal justice system may not be in equilibrium now, but will payments to one component seriously contribute to more instability? Theoretically, one can infer that subsidies, by lowering costs to the organization, will result in an oversupply of the good or service being produced if other conditions remain the same. Poorly conceived and applied, a subsidy formula may reward inefficient jails, increase the flow of persons to already crowded state prisons, or increase incarceration rates.

Summary

Research on the social cost of jails, relative resource allocations internal to their operation, optimum scale of plant, and subsidy effects should produce descriptive economic information that is of immediate relevance to public officials faced with difficult policy choices. Whether a social institution that touches one to two million persons annually will receive priority treatment remains to be seen. The Danish philosopher Kirkegaard has called despair a "sickness unto death"; its antidote, hope!

Appendixes

Appendix A:
Standards by Cost-Center
Function

Variable Number	Short Title	Standards
	1. Plant:	
101	Quarters	Sleeping and living areas shall be designed to provide comfortable and healthful confinement, reasonable prisoner-to-prisoner privacy, constructive interpersonal relationship opportunities, continuous surveillance and protection for prisoners and staff.
102		Single occupancy cells shall have a minimum of 72 square feet with not less than 8 foot ceilings. In no event shall a single occupancy cell contain less than 50 feet of clear floor space.
103		Dormitories for 8 or more occupants shall allow 60 square feet floor space per prisoner and have not less than 10 foot ceilings.
104	Activities	Detention and correction facilities shall provide indoor program and recreation area(s) and may provide or arrange for a multipurpose outdoor exercise and activity area—Consider: 1. Recreation area
105		2. Educational program area
106		3. Library area/facility
107	Feeding	When kitchen facilities are included in a jail such facilities shall be adequate for the sanitary preparation of three nutritionally balanced meals per day. Kitchen facilities and equipment shall meet the requirements of WAC 248-84.
108		Dining area shall allow conversational opportunities in comfortable and pleasant surroundings, meals shall not be served in cells except where necessary for health and well-being of prisoner.
109	Medical	Detention and correction facilities may provide space to be used as a medical examining room. This space may be a multipurpose room. When used as an examining room, it shall provide sight and sound privacy and should be equipped with natural spectrum fluorescent lighting and sufficient lockable storage for medical equipment, supplies, and drugs.
110		When an infirmary is located within a jail, infirmary space shall allow a minimum of 3 feet from the walls, other beds, or any fixed obstruction in the exception that the head of the bed may be against a wall. An infirmary shall have its own lavatory, toilet, shower, and bathtub.
111		If medical isolation facilities are located within jail, such facilities shall contain a lavatory with either foot, knee, wrist, or elbow control and shall have its own adjoining bathing facility and toilet.

As referenced throughout the report, standards are classified according to their cost implications: KC, capital cost; PC, personnel cost; NC, no cost.

Variable Number	Short Title	Standards
112	Visiting	Space for visitation shall be included in detention and correction facilities. Such space shall allow random staff surveillance and the degree of control over physical contact deemed necessary by prisoner classification and shall simultaneously provide comfortable setting for prisoners and their visitors.
113		Detention and correction facilities shall provide space for confidential consultation.
114	Laundry	If laundry facilities are provided within the jail, such facilities shall be adequate for sanitary washing and drying and shall include an area for soiled linens and sorting and a separate area for the storage of clean items.
115	Storage	Detention and correction facilities shall include one or more secure storage area(s) for the storage of prisoners personal clothing and property.
116	Offices	Sufficient space and equipment for administrative and administrative support functions shall be provided in an area secure from prisoner access and from uncontrolled access by the general public.
117	Booking/reception	Booking area(s) and entrance(s) to the receiving area(s) shall be safe and secure. Such area(s) shall include but not be limited to restroom facilities with shower, a strip-search room, holding cell(s), telephone, and space for photographing, fingerprinting, delousing and intoxication determination.
128	Trustee housing	Prisoners who are allowed to go outside the jail regularly shall live and dine in areas separate from and inaccessible to medium- or maximum-security confinement sections or prisoners.

2. *Electric:*

118	Quarters	Prisoners living areas, inspection corridors, and vestibules shall have secure lights with outside switch control. No electrical conduit shall be accessible from any cell, though each living unit may contain outlets and switches provided they are unilaterally controllable by staff.
119	Security/illumination	Illumination at all times shall be adequate for security and surveillance and shall be sufficient (daytime and evening) to permit prisoners to read in their cells.
127	Emergency power	All detention and correction facilities shall be equipped with emergency power sources with sufficient capacity to maintain communications and alarm systems, move one jail elevator if one is present in the jail and to provide minimum lighting within the facility and its perimeter.

Variable Number	*Short Title*	*Standards*
120	3. *Water:*	There shall be an adequate supply of sanitary hot and cold water available at all times. Hot water for general use shall be between 110 and 140 degrees F.
	4. *Heating/ventilation:*	
121 122 123	Temperature	The heating system shall maintain minimum temperature as follows: living quarters, 68°; indoor recreation and misc. areas, 64°; indoor work areas, 60°.
124	Ventilation	The ventilating system shall provide air changes as required by the *Uniform Building Code.*
125	Air conditioning	Jail facilities located in areas having extreme high temperatures in excess of 12 days per year shall have air conditioning.
	5. *Administration/ staffing:*	
129	Org. chart/manual	The department of corrections or the chief law enforcement officer of all jails shall develop and maintain an organizational chart and an operations manual of policies and procedures.
130	Staff sex	At all times in all jails, at least one staff member of the same sex as the prisoner(s) shall be awake, alert, and directly responsible for supervision and surveillance.
131	Surveillance	There shall be continuous sight and/or sound surveillance of all prisoners. Such surveillance may be by remote means provided there is the ability of staff to respond face-to-face to any prisoner within 3 minutes and further provided that a staff member shall personally observe persons confined at least each 60 minutes.
132	Observation	Staff shall be constantly alert to prisoner depression, dissension, family rejection, loneliness, resistance to staff or programs, and the effects of use of substances prohibited by facility rules or by law.
133	Training	All detention and correction facility personnel shall receive pre- and in-service training.
	6. *Records:*	
134		Individual prisoner records include: 1. Admission and release
135		2. Health records
136		3. Other
137		4. Confidentiality
138		5. Prisoner access to jail record
139		6. Transfer of records
140	Incident report	Each department of corrections or chief law enforcement officer shall maintain a written record of all incidents which result in property damage or bodily harm, or serious threat of property damage or bodily harm. Major infraction reports and disciplinary actions shall become part of the prisoner's jail record.

Variable Number	Short Title	Standards
141	Log	All jails shall keep a log of daily activity within the facility.
142	Fiscal/inmate accounting	Each detention and correction facility shall maintain fiscal records which clearly indicate facility operation and maintenance costs according to general accepted accounting principles and shall establish a prisoner population accounting system which reflects the daily population and a complete breakdown by confinement categories.
143	Staff	Performance and training records shall be maintained for each staff member employed by a detention or correction facility.
144	7. Admission:	The receiving officer shall determine that the arrest and placement of each prisoner is being accomplished by a duly authorized officer and a copy of all documents that purport to legally authorize the confinement shall become part of the prisoner's jail record.
145		If only one jail facility officer is on duty, the delivery officer shall remain until the prisoner is locked into the confinement area.
146		A staff member of the same sex as the prisoner shall be present during admission and shall conduct the search.
149		The admission process shall be completed promptly unless the physical condition of the prisoner necessitates delay.
147	Records	The admission form common to all jails shall be completed.
155		The admitting officer shall record and store the prisoner's personal property and issue the prisoner a witnessed receipt.
157		Front and side-view identification photographs of each prisoner shall stipulate the arresting agency and the date of arrest and copies of fingerprints shall be forwarded to the proper state and federal authorities.
150	Search/examination	Each prisoner shall be searched for contraband.
151		The strip search of each prisoner shall include a thorough visual check for birthmarks, cuts, wounds, sores, bruises, scars and injuries, "health tags" and body vermin. All physical marking and "health tag" identifications shall be recorded and made immediately available to the appropriate jail employees and the medical professionals responsible for care of the prisoner. If feasible and particularly when force has been used during arrest, all visible injuries shall be photographed.
152		Any person with body vermin shall be treated appropriately.
153		Complaints of illness or injury shall be checked promptly by a qualified medical professional.

Variable Number	Short Title	Standards
154		A prisoner suspected of having a communicable disease shall be isolated without delay. Arrangements shall be made for his immediate transfer to a facility equipped to handle the suspected disease unless the admitting facility can safely and effectively segregate and maintain the medically prescribed treatment.
156	Personal items	At the discretion of the department of corrections or the chief law enforcement officer, the prisoner may wear clothes provided by the facility or his own clothing.
158		On completion of admission, the prisoner shall be given clean bedding, towel, and other necessary personal-care items.
159		Upon prisoner request, a reasonable supply of writing material shall be furnished.
148	Orientation	Each prisoner, after completion of booking, shall be advised of his right to and be allowed to complete at least two local or collect calls to persons of his choice who may be able to come to his assistance (attorney, immediate family, etc.). If the prisoner chooses not to place the calls allowed, this information shall be noted on the booking form.
160		As soon after booking as possible, each prisoner shall receive an oral orientation. Orientation should include available information regarding the prisoner's confinement and answers to any questions the prisoner may have.
161		In accordance with Section 28 of the 1975 City and County Jails Act, during oral orientation, each prisoner shall be advised of his responsibilities and facility rules and privileges.
162	Housing	Prior to a classification determination, each prisoner shall be confined in a single-occupancy cell whenever possible.
	8. Classification:	
163	General	A classification committee consisting of at least three staff shall be established for classification of prisoners sentenced to that facility. The department of correction or chief law enforcement officer shall establish a classification procedure for each detention facility.
164		Whenever possible, no less than two detention facility staff members shall be responsible for classification determinations.
165		For each prisoner sentenced to that facility, those responsible for classification shall determine degree of security required, cell assignment, program eligibility, and regulations for association within and outside the confinement area.

Variable Number	Short Title	Standards
166		As explained elsewhere in these standards, persons responsible for classification determinations shall also hear disciplinary cases, review literature screening appeals, and recommend diminution of sentence and alternatives to confinement.
299		With the concurrence of the department of corrections or chief law enforcement officer, the disciplinary hearing body may recommend an alternative to confinement to the court of jurisdiction.
167	Procedure	Each prisoner sentenced to that facility shall be interviewed by persons responsible for classification determinations.
168		The prisoner shall be informed of the classification cell-assignment decision and the basis for that decision.
169		A prisoner dissatisfied by a cell-assignment decision shall have the right to request a review of the decision by the department of corrections or chief law enforcement officer.
170		Because classification is an ongoing process, a procedure to reclassification shall be developed and each prisoner informed of the conditions prerequisite for reclassification.
171	Criteria	Criteria for prisoner classification includes: 1. Age
172		2. Sex
173		3. Special problem prisoner
174		4. Minimum security prisoner
175		5. Other criteria
	9. Release:	
176	Identification	The releasing officer shall positively determine prisoner identity and ascertain that there is legal authority for the release.
177		The release form common to all jails shall be completed.
180		In addition to the release procedures designated above, the releasing officer shall determine that the receiving unit or person has the authority to accept custody.
178	Property receipt	All prisoners being released shall sign a witnessed receipt for personal property returned.
179	Physical examination	Each prisoner being discharged shall receive a visual body check to detect changes from his admitting physical record.
181	Body	In cooperation with the county coroner, each facility shall establish procedures for release of a prisoner's body and personal property.

Variable Number	Short Title	Standards
	10. Transportation	
182	Security	Vehicles for the transportation of prisoners considered dangerous shall have a divider between the driver's seat and other seat areas.
183		Prisoners being transported may be handcuffed, placed in a restraining belt or handcuffed to other prisoners of the same sex. Related prisoners of the opposite sex may be handcuffed together.
184		No prisoner shall be handcuffed to a vehicle.
185		Prisoner shall not be left in an unattended or unsupervised vehicle.
186		A female shall accompany any female prisoner in transport and a male officer shall accompany any male prisoner.
	11. Security and control:	
187	General	All jails shall establish a positive means of identifying prisoners.
188		Perimeter security shall be maintained.
189		Security devices shall be maintained in proper working condition at all times.
190		No prisoner shall be permitted to have authority over other prisoners.
191		Detention and correction facilities shall develop a system for taking and recording prisoner counts. This procedure shall be followed at shift changes and at other regular or irregular times.
192	Contraband	Any item or person entering or leaving a jail shall be subject to search.
193		When housed in a jail facility, work-release prisoners and prisoners who have regular contact outside the jail shall not be permitted contact with other prisoner classifications or entrance to areas frequented by other prisoners.
194		There shall be irregularly scheduled searches for contraband in detention and correction facilities. Conspicuously posted signs shall display the statutory penalty for giving or arranging to give anything to a prisoner without official authorization.
195		Non-English-speaking visitors shall be informed of the statutory penalty whether verbally or by posted signs in the appropriate language.
196	"Hot" items	Weapons and keys to weapon lockers shall not be permitted in confinement and booking areas.
197		Key regulations shall be established by the department of corrections or chief law enforcement officer and read and initialed by all staff.

Variable Number	Short Title	Standards
198		A control point shall be designated for key cataloging and logging the distribution of keys.
199		There shall be at least two sets of jail facility keys; one set in use and the other stored for use in the event of an emergency.
200		All keys not in use shall be stored in a secure key locker inaccessible to prisoners.
201		Emergency keys shall be "red tagged" and placed in the designated emergency section of the key locker.
202		Inside and outside keys shall be maintained on separate rings and no staff member shall carry both simultaneously.
203		Keys shall be accounted for at all times and the distribution certified at each shift change.
204		Jail facility keys shall never be issued to a prisoner.
205	Equipment	Protective equipment, tear gas, and any other chemical suppressing agent shall be kept in a secure area, inaccessible to prisoners and unauthorized persons, but quickly accessible to officers of the facility.
206		All kitchen utensils and tools shall be marked for identification, recorded and kept in a secure place; also, toxic substances shall be kept in locked storage and use of toxic substances shall be strictly supervised.
207	Emergency procedures	The department of corrections or the chief law enforcement officer shall formulate comprehensive written emergency procedures relative to escapes, riots, rebellions, assaults, injuries, suicides or attempted suicides, outbreak of infectious disease, fire, acts of nature and any other type of major disaster or disturbance. The emergency plans shall outline the responsibilities of jail facility staff, evacuation procedures, and subsequent disposition of the prisoners after removal from the area or facility. Such plan shall be formulated in cooperation with the appropriate supporting local government units.
208		Emergency plans shall always be available to the officer in charge of the jail and all personnel shall always be aware of and trained in the procedures.
209		All serious incidents and emergencies shall be reported to the City and County Jail Commission on forms provided and at times prescribed by the commission.
210		Only lawful and reasonable force to the person of a prisoner shall be used. Such force shall be used only after obtaining the prior approval of the senior jail officer on duty and a record of the event shall be made in the jail log. Only in cases of self-defense, to prevent escape, to prevent injury to a person (including the prisoner himself) or to prevent the commission of a crime shall prior approval not be necessary for the use of such force. The extent of such force

Variable Number	Short Title	Standards
		shall always be limited to the extent it is reasonably necessary to accomplish its purpose.
211	Deprivation of personal items	Prisoners shall not be deprived of their clothes, blankets, or personal-care items unless there is probable cause to believe that the prisoner will misuse such articles to damage property, inflict bodily harm (to himself or others), or substantially compromise the security of the jail. Such deprivation shall be used and continued only if there is no other practicable way to control the prisoner.
	12. Discipline:	
212	Written	The department of corrections or chief law enforcement officer shall establish uniform rules and disciplinary sanctions to guide the conduct of all prisoners.
213	Posted	In addition to the oral orientation, printed rules, and possible disciplinary sanctions shall be posted conspicuously throughout the jail. Non-English-speaking prisoners shall be informed of the rules either verbally or by posted signs in the appropriate language.
215	Procedures	Minor violations of the rules may be handled informally by any staff member by reprimand, warning or minor sanction as defined by local rules. Such incidents may become part of the prisoners record only with the approval of the supervisor and verbal notification to the prisoner.
214		All major infractions of the rules shall be reported in writing to the supervisor prior to shift change by the staff member observing or discovering the act. Such reports shall become part of the prisoner's jail record.
216		Discipline plan for major infractions include:
		1. Disciplinary hearing
217		2. Procedures
218	Sanctions	Nonpunitive corrective action shall be the first consideration in all disciplinary proceedings.
219		When punitive measures are imposed, such measures shall be in accordance with law, appropriate to the severity of the infraction, and based on considerations of the individual involved.
220		Acceptable forms of discipline shall consist of the following:
		1. Loss of privileges
221		2. Removal from work detail or other assignments
222		3. Recommendation of forfeiture of "good time" credit
223		4. Transfer to the maximum security or segregation section
224	Limitations	No prisoner or group of prisoners shall be given authority to administer punishment to any other prisoner or group of prisoners.

Variable Number	Short Title	Standards
225		Deviation from normal feeding procedures shall not be used as a disciplinary sanction.
226		Deprivation of clothing, bed, bedding, or normal hygienic implements and facilities shall not be used as a disciplinary sanction.
227		Correspondence privileges shall not be denied or restricted, except in cases where the prisoner has violated correspondence regulations. In no case shall the correspondence privilege with any member of the Bar, holder of public office, the courts, or the department of corrections or chief law enforcement officer be suspended.
228		Visitation privileges shall not be denied or restricted as a sanction for infractions of rules of the institution unrelated to visitation. Under no circumstances shall attorney/client visits be restricted.
229		No prisoner shall be held in disciplinary segregation for more than 5 consecutive days without review by the disciplinary hearing body or chief law enforcement officer and in no event shall a prisoner be held in disciplinary segregation for more than 10 consecutive days as the result of any one hearing.
230		Corporal punishment and physical restraint (handcuffs, leather restraints, straitjackets, etc.) shall not be used as sanctions. Reasonable physical restraint when necessary for medical reasons shall be medically directed, except that in an emergency reasonable physical restraint may be used to control a grossly disturbed or violent prisoner, but medical review and direction shall be promptly obtained.
	13. Health care:	
233	Exams	During the booking process in all jails, a member of the jail staff shall conduct an initial health screening to detect signs of injury and/or symptoms of illness. Jail staff shall obtain a brief health history at booking from prisoners who need immediate or early medical or other health care. Such prisoner shall promptly receive the appropriate attention.
234		When the need for immediate or early care is not apparent, detention and correction facility staff shall obtain a brief history within 12 hours after booking. Within 48 hours of admission (exclusive of Sundays), each prisoner's health history shall be reviewed and assessed by a qualified doctor, nurse, or paramedic. If health care is needed, the qualified medical professional shall establish a plan to provide the appropriate and feasible care.
232	Records	Health records shall be maintained as specified in the Recommended Minimum Standards.

Variable Number	Short Title	Standards
231	Care	All jails shall provide health care and medical services in accordance with Sections 29, 30, and 32 of the 1975 City and County Jail Act.
235		Use of and coordinating with health care support agencies in the community is recommended and encouraged.
237		All medications shall be securely stored, given only upon prescription by a physician and issued only by an officer at the time of use. The issuing officer shall observe that the medicine is taken as directed.
236		Every jail shall have written, physician approved delousing procedures. Such procedures shall be consistent with suggested procedures issued by the Washington State Department of Social and Health Services.
238		Each jail shall provide or arrange for medical isolation facilities for prisoners with communicable diseases. Communicable diseases shall be determined by a qualified medical professional.
239		All detention and correction facility staff shall receive first-aid training prior to employment or during the probationary period.
	14. *Food:*	
244	Menus	Menus shall be prepared by the jail facility staff and reviewed by the local county health department, the county extension service, or other qualified nutrition consultant available in the community. Nutrition and intake includes: 1. Preparation
245		2. Serving
246		3. Quality
247		4. Quantity
248		Diets shall approximate the dietary allowances specified by the food and nutrition board of the National Research Council adjusted to age, sex, and activity.
249		Diets ordered by medical staff shall be strictly observed.
240	Medical diets	At least three meals a day shall be served at regular intervals. The morning meal shall be served within 14 hours of the previous day's evening meal.
241	Service	Holding and detention facilities may arrange for prepared meal service or serve frozen, packaged meals, provided these meals conform to the nutritional requirements set forth in paragraph above.
242		Meals shall be served in a reasonable manner; hot food served hot, cold food served cold.
243		Prisoner meals shall be served on compartmented steel or heat-resistant plastic trays. Stainless steel or plastic eating utensils shall be provided.
250	Sanitation	Food service operations in jails shall conform to the sanitation rules and regulations set forth in WAC 248-84.

Variable Number	Short Title	Standards
251	Staff permit	In detention and correction facilities a paid staff member, responsible for kitchen supervision and food preparation, shall obtain a food and beverage workers permit. Under supervision of this staff member, prisoners may assist in the kitchen and need not acquire a food and beverage workers permit.
	15. Personal care items:	
252	Clothing	Provision shall be made for separate insect-proof clothing storage to prevent migration of lice from infested clothing.
253		Prisoners shall be issued clean outer garments at least once a week. Undergarments and socks shall be issued more frequently.
254		If prisoners are required to wear clothing issued by the facility, detention and correction facilities shall, as necessary, clean and sanitize personal clothing prior to storage.
255	Bedding	Prisoners shall be issued clean bed linens and mattress covers upon arrival and at least once a week thereafter.
256		Mattresses shall have a washable ticking or cover and shall be sanitized at least semi-annually.
257		Blankets shall be washed at frequent intervals to maintain a clean condition, but at least once every 60 days, and always before reissue.
258	Personnel	Personal-care items issued to each prisoner in detention and correction facilities shall include, but not be limited to, soap, towel, toothpaste or powder, toothbrush and comb. Female prisoners shall be supplied with necessary feminine hygiene items.
259		Each prisoner shall have his own drinking cup or fountain.
260		Prisoners may be permitted to have a reasonable number of additional personal items.
	16. Sanitation and safety:	
261	General cleaning and daily inspection	All jails shall be kept in a clean and sanitary condition, free from any accumulation of dirt, filth, rubbish, garbage, or other matter detrimental to health.
262		The housekeeping program shall include a daily general sanitation inspection and daily removal of trash and garbage.
263	Prisoners/clean	Each prisoner shall clean his own living area daily and may voluntarily clear other space within the confinement area.
264	Insects/rodents/pets	Insects and rodents shall be eliminated by safe and effective means. Prisoners shall be removed from areas in which insecticides and rodenticides are being used.

Variable Number	Short Title	Standards
265		Pets shall not be allowed in jail facilities.
266	Laundry	Each jail shall have adequate laundry facilities or shall contract laundry services with a commercial laundry.
267	Fire	The department of correction or chief law enforcement officer shall consult with the local fire department having jurisdiction over the facility in developing a fire-suppression plan which shall include, but not be limited to: A. A fire prevention plan to be part of the operations manual of policies and procedures
268		B. Regular fire-prevention inspection by facility staff
269		C. Fire-prevention inspections at least biennially by the fire department having jurisdiction. Recommendations resulting from inspections shall be promptly implemented
270		D. A regular schedule for testing and servicing fire-suppression equipment (extinguishers, hoses, etc.)
126	Detection/ suppression	All jails shall have smoke and fire-detection and fire-alarm systems. All jails shall have fire-suppression equipment (extinguishers) available to staff, but secured from prisoners.

17. *Services:*

Variable Number	Short Title	Standards
271	Personal	The department of corrections or chief law enforcement officer of each detention or correction facility shall either establish, maintain and operate a commissary or provide prisoners with a printed list of approved items to be purchased at least once a week at local stores.
272		Commissary items shall include books, periodicals, and newspapers.
273		Proceeds from a jail facility store shall be used for operation and maintenance of the commissary service or for prisoner welfare expenses.
274		If prisoners are not permitted to keep money on their person, payments for commissary purchases shall be made by debit on the prisoner's cash account. All expenditures from a prisoner's account shall be accurately recorded and receipted.
275		All jails shall make arrangements for reasonable barber or beauty shop services.
276	Library service	In conjunction with state and/or local library service units, each jail shall make provisions for library services.
277	Legal assistance	All detention and correction facilities shall provide access to law books and other materials requested by a prisoner in his preparation for legal proceedings.
278		Facility rules shall not prohibit one prisoner from assisting another in the preparation of legal papers.

Variable Number	Short Title	Standards
279	Religious services	Upon request from a prisoner, the jail facility shall arrange religious services.
280		Detention and correction facilities with an average daily population of 25 or more shall arrange for weekly religious services.
281		To the extent possible, prisoners shall be permitted to observe religious holidays and receive sacraments of their faith.
282		Attendance at religious services shall be voluntary and prisoners who do not wish to hear or participate shall not be exposed to such services.
283	Counseling	Counseling services shall be available to provide prisoners in detention and correction facilities with an opportunity to discuss their problems, interests, and programs.
284		The department of corrections or chief law enforcement officer may utilize voluntary counseling resources available in the community.
285		To the extent possible, professionals shall serve in an advisory capacity when jail facility personnel or community volunteers engage in counseling.
286		Counselors may submit written recommendations to the chief law enforcement officer or disciplinary review body.
287		Counseling services shall be voluntarily received unless ordered by the appropriate court or the disciplinary review body.
288		To the extent possible, prisoners being discharged shall receive assistance in obtaining employment, housing, acceptable clothing, and transportation.
289	Work program	The department of corrections or chief law enforcement officer shall establish work programs in accordance with Section 11 and 36 of the 1975 City and County Jails Act.
290	Education/training	The department of corrections or chief law enforcement officer of each correction facility shall arrange for the development of an education and training program, utilizing local school districts, colleges, trade schools, unions, industry, interested citizens, and other available community, state, and federal resources.
291		Paid staff member(s) shall have designated responsibility for supervision of the education and training programs.
292		Correspondence courses shall be available at the prisoner's request and expense.
293		Correction facilities shall provide courses to prepare qualified prisoners for the "General Education Development" test.

Variable Number	Short Title	Standards
294	Detention	Each detention facility shall provide courses to prepare qualified prisoners for the "General Education Development" test.
295		Detention facilities shall encourage participation in other education and training programs available locally.
296	Leisure	To the extent possible, detention, and correction facilities shall provide opportunities for all prisoners to participate in leisure-time activities of their choice and abilities. Such activities may include athletic programs, hobbies and crafts, table games, radio and television, motion pictures, cards, puzzles, checkers, and chess.
297		Detention and correction facilities shall arrange for at least one hour of physical exercise per day.
298		Volunteers may be used to plan and supervise exercise programs and other leisure-time activities, but paid staff member(s) shall have designated responsibility for supervision of such programs.
	18. Communication:	
300	General	Communication between prisoners and persons outside any jail and communication between prisoners and staff shall be encouraged for purposes of retaining constructive community relationships, stimulating intellectual pursuits, assisting in the attainment of vocational or educational goals and facilitating legal inquiries. Communication is deemed a right rather than a privilege and can be abridged only when there is probable cause to believe that facility security or the welfare of the prisoners or staff is endangered.
301	Staff	Communication from prisoner to staff shall be encouraged and respected.
302		Requests for an audience with staff shall be honored as soon as reasonably possible.
303	Telephone	Facility rules shall specify regular telephone usage times and the maximum length of calls (not to be less than 5 minutes).
304		Telephone usage hours shall include time during the normal day and time during the evening.
305		Except for a reasonable number of telephone calls to a prisoner's attorney, pastor, employer, or immediate family, calls shall be at the prisoner's expense. All long distance calls shall be collect.
306		Location of telephone facilities shall insure reasonable privacy and telephone calls shall not be monitored, tape-recorded, or spotchecked except by court order.
307		Reasons for calls shall be the personal concern of the prisoner, except in consideration of requests for emergency calls beyond normal telephone hours.

Variable Number	Short Title	Standards
308	Periodicals	Prisoners shall be permitted to subscribe to and otherwise receive books, newspapers and periodicals. Books, newspapers, and periodicals may be denied a prisoner only if such denial furthers one or more of the substantial governmental interests of security against escape or unauthorized entry.
309		When a publication is withheld from a prisoner for the reasons set forth above, the prisoner shall then receive: A. Immediate written ·notice that the publication is being denied, accompanied by an explanation of the reason(s) of the denial
310		B. A reasonable opportunity to appeal that decision to the disciplinary hearing body, the department of corrections, or the chief law enforcement officer. The prisoner shall be promptly informed of the right of appeal and shall be provided a form on which a written appeal may be submitted
311		C. A written decision on the appeal of the denial including the reason(s) for the denial.
312	1-day delay mail	Incoming or outgoing mail shall be retained no more than one day.
313	Unlimited mail	Except in the case of prisoners without funds, prisoners shall be permitted to mail out any number of letters. Prisoners without funds shall be permitted to mail up to 3 letters per calendar week at public expense or with postage purchased from the prisoner welfare fund, provided upon proper showing the number may be increased. Such prisoners may mail out any number of letters to their attorneys, the courts, elected federal, state, and county officials. There shall be no restriction on the identity of the prisoners' correspondence.
314	Unlimited receipt	No restriction shall be placed on the number of letters a prisoner may receive.
315	Detainees' mail	Failing an order from a court of competent jurisdiction, outgoing mail of pretrial detainees (prisoners not on parole hold, not subject to probation revocation, or not currently under sentence) shall be neither opened nor read.
316		Incoming mail of pretrial detainees (as described above) may be opened only for the purpose of inspecting for contraband and afterwards shall be delivered directly and immediately to the addressee. Such mail shall not be read. Whenever feasible, it is recommended that this mail be opened in the presence of the addressee.
317	Postconviction	Outgoing mail shall not be opened unless the department of corrections or chief law enforcement officer has probable cause to believe that the content of a specific letter presents a clear and present danger to

Variable Number	Short Title	Standards
		institutional security and/or is in violation of postal regulations.
318		Incoming mail shall not be read or censored, but may be opened and inspected for contraband, cash, and checks. Mail shall be resealed and delivered to the addressee.
319		Contraband which is not illegal may be destroyed upon the prisoner's written request or returned collect to the sender.
320		Dangerous or illegal contraband and the accompanying letter shall be turned over to proper authorities.
321		A receipt for permissible items received in letters, including money and checks, shall be signed by the prisoner, a staff member, and a witness.
322		When a prisoner is prohibited from sending a letter, the letter and a written and signed notice stating the reason for disapproval and indicating the portion(s) of the letter causing disapproval shall be given the prisoner.
323		When a prisoner is prohibited from receiving a letter, the letter and a written signed notice stating the reasons for denial and indicating the portion(s) of the letter causing the denial shall be given the sender. The prisoner shall be given notice in writing that the letter has been prohibited, indicating the reason(s) and the sender's name.
324		When a prisoner is prohibited from sending or receiving mail, the prisoner shall be given: 1. A reasonable opportunity to appeal the decision to the disciplinary review body, the department of corrections, or the chief law enforcement officer. The prisoner shall be promptly informed of the right to appeal and shall be provided a form on which a written appeal may be submitted 2. Written decision on the action on the appeal of the denial, including the reasons for the denial.
325		Incoming mail of postconviction prisoners that is clearly marked as coming from an attorney, court, elected federal, state, or county official, or prisoner assistance organization shall be opened only in the presence of the addressee. Other incoming mail indicating on its face that it is to be opened in the presence of the addressee shall be so opened.
326		Mail to or from attorney, court, elected federal, state, or county officials, and prisoner assistance groups shall not be read.
327		There shall be no additional restrictions on prisoner correspondence for disciplinary or punishment purposes unless the prisoner has violated rules as to correspondence. Upon proper showing of the alleged violation, the prisoner's mail may be restricted for a limited time, but such restriction shall not apply to attorney/client mail or correspondence with the court.

Variable Number	Short Title	Standards
328	Packages	If a facility allows prisoners to receive packages, all packages shall be opened and inspected.
329		Packages may be received only if the contents conform to rules adopted by the department of corrections or chief law enforcement officer and a witnessed receipt for permissible items shall be completed at the time of delivery to the addressee.
330		Outgoing packages shall be inspected and mailed at the prisoner's expense.
331	Visitation	Open visitation shall be allowed whenever feasible, but prisoners requiring greater security shall be provided with visiting facilities which do not allow physical contact.
332		The degree of security required for each prisoner during visitation shall be determined by those persons responsible for classification.
342		Signs giving notice that all visitors and their accompanying possessions are subject to search shall be conspicuously posted at the entrances to the facility and at the entrance of the visiting area.
343		Any person may refuse a search but subsequent to such refusal may then be denied entrance.
344		Other reasons for denying entrance to visitors shall include, but not be limited to: A. An attempt, or reasonable suspicion of an attempt to bring contraband into the facility
345		B. Obvious use of alcohol or controlled substances
346		C. Request from the prisoner's physician
347		D. Request from the prisoner
348		Whenever a visitor is refused admittance, the prisoner shall receive notice of the refusal.
333	Social	Facility rules shall specify regular social visiting hours.
334		Each prisoner shall be allowed a minimum of 3 hours total visitation per week in detention and correction facilities.
335		Immediate family (wives, husbands, children, parents, brothers, sisters, grandparents, aunts, and uncles) by consanguinity or affinity shall be given preference for allotted visitation time unless the prisoner specifies otherwise.
336		Friends shall be allowed to visit during established visiting hours at the discretion of the department of corrections or chief law enforcement officer and the prisoner.
337		Except for immediate family members, visitors 17 years of age and under shall be accompanied by a parent or guardian.
338		The department of corrections or chief law enforce-

Variable Number	Short Title	Standards
		ment officer may grant special visitation privileges to visitors who have traveled long distances, to visitors for hospital prisoners, and for other unusual circumstances.
339	Business/ professional	Each prisoner shall be allowed confidential visits from his attorney or pastor.
340		By prior arrangement with the jail staff, a prisoner shall be allowed confidential visits by his employer, doctor, dentist, tax consultant, banker, investment, or insurance broker, with educators from a bona fide school or job-training facility and with employment consultants from recognized firms.
341		Law enforcement professionals shall be allowed to interview prisoners at reasonable times and with prior notice, unless it appears circumstances do not permit delay.

Source: Washington State City and County Jail Commission, *Report to the Washington State Legislature* (1974). Grouping by cost center function performed by the Correctional Economics Center, 1975.

Appendix B:
The BARS System

The Washington State Auditor's Office devised the Budgeting, Accounting and Reporting System to facilitate standardization of accounting procedures among local governments. Budgets are classified by main expenditure categories, within which more detailed subobjects are accounted:

Personnel services (BARS code 10)
    Salaries and wages
    Overtime and hazardous duty
    Personnel benefits
    Uniforms and clothing

Supplies (BARS code 20)
    Office supplies
    Operating supplies

Other services and charges (BARS code 30)
    Professional services
    Repairs and maintenance
    Rentals

Capital outlays (BARS code 60)
    Improvements other than buildings
    Machinery and equipment
    Construction projects

Ideally, budgetary data for each jail would exist for all subobjects permitting some degree of cost accounting by functional area. However, because the BARS system has only recently been implemented, several counties and cities are currently transforming their accounting procedures. Regional variations may still exist among definitions of objects and subobjects. Additionally, smaller jurisdictions need not report as much detail. Some of the more significant problems resulting from misunderstandings about account definitions and difficulties in altering traditional local accounting procedures were:

1. Salaries paid for contracted professional services are included not in this expenditure group but in "other services." The personnel object category tends to understate manpower costs to the extent medical, legal, or other professional services are not included. When medical services are performed by a jail staff member, medical salaries are contained in "personal services."

2. Operating supplies were intended to include such items as food, drugs,

institutional cleaning supplies, and blankets. Many jurisdictions included only food, the most costly subobject, and entered other operating supplies as miscellaneous items.

3. Other services and charges are defined as services other than personal services that are required by the jail to perform assigned functions that jail staff cannot provide. The relevant services include:

Professional services—medical, dental, hospital, legal, custodial, and cleaning services

Communication—telephone and postage

Public utility services—heating, electricity, water, and waste removal

Repairs and maintenance—labor and supplies required for services such as painting, plumbing, and electrical repairs

Miscellaneous—incorporates a range of services that may include laundry services, fees, and unclassified contractual services.

Within the services category, several problems arose in attempts to estimate comparable jail costs. First, medical services are not always included. Their exclusion occurs when the service is provided gratis by the community or by the county health department. Although not incurred directly by the jail, they are legitimate operating costs and should be included in any estimate of total costs. Utilities charges are not always identifiable because the majority of jails are located in county courthouses or city police departments. Attempting to derive true utilities costs for these jails was often impossible or resulted in estimates that were tenuous at best. To maintain comparability, these costs were excluded throughout the analysis.

4. Capital outlays include purchases that are related to building and equipment: costs incidental to construction, major repairs, and remodeling; purchase of machinery and equipment, such as washing machines and dishwashers; and books and library materials. Most jurisdictions in Washington State did not enter capital expenditures properly and greatly understated operating costs. Appropriate adjustments were made for the Correctional Economics Center analysis.

Appendix C: Cost Impact of Standards by BARS Categories[a]

No.	Standards and Short Subtitles	Person-nel (BARS-10)	Supplies Of-fice (BARS-21)	Opera-tions (BARS-22)	Ser-vices (BARS-30)	Plant (BARS-62)	Equip-ment (BARS-64)
	1. *Plant*						
101	Quarters:						X
102	Single					X	X
103	Dorm					X	
	Activities:						
104	Educational	X				X	
105	Recreational	X				X	
106	Library					X	
	Feeding:						
107	Kitchen					X	X
108	Dining	X				X	X
	Medical:						
109	Examining	X				X	X
110	Infirmary					X	X
111	Isolation					X	X
	Visiting:						
112	Social					X	X
113	Professional					X	
114	Laundry					X	X
115	Storage					X	X
116	Offices					X	X
117	Booking/reception		X		X	X	X
128	Trustee housing	X				X	X
	2. *Electrical*						
118	Quarters:			X		X	X
119	Security/illumination			X		X	X
127	Emergency power			X		X	X
120	3. *Water*			X		X	X
	4. *Heating/ventilation*						
	Temperatures:						
121	Living			X		X	X
122	Indoor recreation			X		X	X
123	Indoor work areas			X		X	X
124	Ventilation			X		X	X
125	Air conditioning		X	X		X	X

[a]Analysis performed by Correctional Economics Center based on meetings with Washington State Jail Commission.

No.	Standards and Short Subtitles	Personnel (BARS-10)	Supplies Office (BARS-21)	Operations (BARS-22)	Services (BARS-30)	Plant (BARS-62)	Equipment (BARS-64)
	5. Administration/staffing						
129	Org. chart/manual						
130	Staff sex	X				X	X
131	Surveillance	X				X	X
132	Observation	X					
133	Training	X	X		X		
	6. Records						
	Prisoner:						
134	A/R		X				
135	Health		X				
136	Other						
137	Confidentiality	X	X				X
138	Access	X	X				
139	Transfer		X				
140	Incident reports		X				
141	Log		X				
142	Fiscal/inmate acctng.	X	X				
143	Staff		X				
	7. Admission						
144	General:						
144	Identification						
145	Lock-up procedure						
146	Same sex	X					
149	Timely process						
	Records:						
147	Admission form		X				
155	Personal property						
157	Photograph		X				X
	Search/examination:						
150	Contraband						
151	Physical condition						
152	Vermin treatment			X			
153	Medical exam				X		
154	Communicable disease		X		X	X	X
	Personal items:						
156	Clothing			X		X	X
158	Bedding			X			
159	Writing			X			
	Orientation:						
148	Phone call				X		

No.	Standards and Short Subtitles	Person-nel (BARS-10)	Supplies		Ser-vices (BARS-30)	Plant (BARS-62)	Equip-ment (BARS-64)
			Of-fice (BARS-21)	Opera-tions (BARS-22)			
160	Oral orientation	X					
161	Rules	X					
162	Housing						
	8. *Classification*						
	General:						
163	Committee	X					
164	Established procedure						
165	Classify	X					
166	Discipline	X					
299	Alternatives						
	Procedure:						
167	Interview	X					
168	Notice	X					
169	Housing appeal	X					
170	Reclassification	X					
	Criteria:						
171	Age	X					
172	Sex	X					
173	Problem	X					
174	Minimum security	X					
175	Other	X					
	9. *Release*						
	Identification:						
176	Prisoner			X			X
177	Form						
180	Jurisdiction						
178	Property receipt						
179	Physical exam						
181	Body						
	10. *Transportation*						
	Security:						
182	Vehicle divider						X
183	Physical restraint						X
184	Prohibit						
185	Not unattended	X					
186	Escort sex	X					
	11. *Security and control*						
	General:						
187	Inmate identification	X	X				X
188	Perimeter security					X	

No.	Standards and Short Subtitles	Person-nel (BARS-10)	Supplies		Ser-vices (BARS-30)	Plant (BARS-62)	Equip-ment (BARS-64)
			Of-fice (BARS-21)	Opera-tions (BARS-22)			
189	Device maintenance				X		X
190	Trustee supervision	X					
191	Courts	X					
	Contraband:						
192	Searches	X					
193	W/R isolation	X		X	X	X	X
194	Shakedown	X					
195	Notice penalty						
	"Hot items":						
196	Weapons/keys storage						
197	Key regulations						
198	Key control						
199	Emergency keys			X			
200	Key storage						X
201	Key tags						
202	Key separation						
203	Key accounting						
204	Issue control						
	Equipment:						
205	Security equipment						X
206	Kitchen tools						X
	Emergency procedure:						
207	Plan						
208	Training	X					
209	Reporting						
210	Force						
211	Depriv. of personal items						
12.	*Discipline*						
212	Written						
213	Posted			X			
	Procedures:						
215	Minor						
215	Major						
216	Major hearing	X					
217	Major procedure	X					
	Sanctions:						
218	Nonpunative						
219	Least drastic						
220	Privileges						
221	Work detail						

No.	Standards and Short Subtitles	Person-nel (BARS-10)	Supplies		Ser-vices (BARS-30)	Plant (BARS-62)	Equip-ment (BARS-64)
			Of-fice (BARS-21)	Opera-tions (BARS-22)			
222	Good Time						
223	Segregation	X				X	X
	Limitations:						
224	No peer group						
225	No food						
226	No personal						
227	No mail						
228	No visitation						
229	5/10-day segments	X					
230	No corporal						
13.	Health care						
	Exams:						
233	Booking screening	X					
234	12-hour screening	X		X	X		
232	Records:	X					
	Care:						
231	Sections 29, 30, 32	X		X			
235	Community agencies	X					
237	Medicine dispensing						X
236	Delousing			X			
238	Isolation/diagnosis	X			X	X	X
239	First-aid training	X			X		
14.	Food						
	Menus:						
	Printed/reviewed	X					
244	Preparation						
245	Serving						
246	Quality						
247	Quantity						
248	Nutrition			X			
249	Medical Diets			X			
	Services:						
240	3 meals/14 hours			X	X		
241	Detention			X	X		
242	Hot/cold			X			X
243	Utensils				X		X
250	Sanitation						
251	Staff permit	X					
15.	Personal Care Items						
	Clothing						
252	Storage			X		X	X
253	Issue			X		X	X
254	Clng./inst. clothing			X		X	X

			Supplies				
No.	Standards and Short Subtitles	Personnel (BARS-10)	Office (BARS-21)	Operations (BARS-22)	Services (BARS-30)	Plant (BARS-62)	Equipment (BARS-64)
	Bedding:						
255	Issue			X			
256	Sanitary/mattress			X	X		
257	Sanitary/blankets			X	X		
	Personnel:						
258	Issue items			X			
259	Water/sanitary			X		X	X
260	Possession of other						
16.	Sanitation and safety						
261	General cleaning			X			X
262	Daily inspections						
263	Prisoners/clean			X			
264	Insects/rodents			X	X		
265	No pets						
266	Laundry facilities				X		X
	Fire:						
267	Plan						
268	Inspection/staff	X					
269	Inspection/fire dept.						
270	Equipment	X					
126	Detection/suppression					X	X
17.	Services						
	Personal:						
271	Commissary/st. access	X					
272	Commissary items						
273	Proceeds usage						
274	Accounting (comm.)	X					
275	Barber/beauty				X		
276	Library services						
	Legal assistance						
277	Access to books						
278	Assistants to pris.						
	Religious services:						
279	Services on request						
280	25+ = weekly services	X			X		
281	Right to worship						
282	Voluntary attendance				X		
	Counseling:						
283	Available	X			X		
284	Use volunteers						
285	Prof. supervision						

No.	Standards and Short Subtitles	Personnel (BARS-10)	Supplies		Services (BARS-30)	Plant (BARS-62)	Equipment (BARS-64)
			Office (BARS-21)	Operations (BARS-22)			
286	Written recommendation						
287	Voluntary					X	
288	Released/assistance	X		X	X		
289	Work program	X					
	Ed./ training corrections:						
290	Community resources	X		X	X	X	
291	Staff supervision	X					
292	Correspondence courses						
293	Courses: GED	X		X	X	X	
	Detention:						
294	Courses: GED	X		X			
295	Community resources						
	Leisure:						
296	Available hobbies			X			X
297	Physical exercise	X				X	X
298	Staff supervision	X					
18.	Communications						
300	General	X					
	Staff:						
301	Encouraged						
302	Audiences permitted						
	Telephone:						
303	Regular usage				X	X	
304	Usage times	X			X	X	
305	$-exempt calls				X	X	
306	Privacy				X	X	
307	Emergency calls				X	X	
	Mail:						
	Periodicals:						
308	Subscpt./recpt.						
309	Notice of denial						
310	Appeal	X					
311	Written appeal des.	X					
312	1-day delay mail						
313	Unlimited mailing				X		
314	Unlimited receipt						
	Detainee's mail:						
315	Not open or read						
316	Inspect for contraband						
	Postconviction:						
317	Out mail/inspection						
318	Incoming mail/insp.						

| No. | Standards and Short Subtitles | Person- nel (BARS- 10) | Supplies | | Ser- vices (BARS- 30) | Plant (BARS- 62) | Equip- ment (BARS- 64) |
			Of- fice (BARS- 21)	Opera- tions (BARS- 22)			
319	Legal contraband						
320	Illegal contraband	X					
321	Receipts	X					
322	Notice/disapproval						
323	Receipt/disapproval						
324	Appeal/disapproval	X					
325	Opening limitations						
326	Opening exemptions						
327	No other restrictions						
	Packages:						
328	All receipts insp.	X					
329	Rules for receipts						
330	Outgoing inspection	X					
	Visitation:						
	General:						
331	Security/contact					X	X
332	Classif. off det. scy.						
342	Notice of search						
343	Refusal of search						
344	Contraband denial						
345	Alcohol denial						
346	Prisoner's physician						
347	Prisoner						
348	Written notice						
	Social:						
333	Hours/times						
334	3 hours/week	X				X	X
335	Preference family						
336	Friends						
337	Under 17 years old						
338	Special visits						
	Business/professional:						
339	Confidential				X		
340	Other confidential				X		
341	Interviews				X		

Appendix D:
Comparative Effects of Weighted Needs on Alternative Estimation Methods[a]

---

[a]Analysis performed by Correctional Economics Center, 1975.

Variables	Type-2 Methods			Type-3 Methods			Type-4 Methods		
	A	B	C	A	B	C	A	B	C
S_s	10.4	10.4	20.5	3.0	3.0	4.6	3.3	3.3	4.6
M_s	3.5	3.5	5.1	57	57	87.4	59.4	59.4	82.8
P_s	24.5	24.5	35.7	39.1	39.1	45.8	43	43	41.3
$P_s - S_s = M$	14.1	14.1	15.2	64%	64%	64%	70%	70%	66%
$\overline{CR}_s$	73%	73%	69%	73%	75%	75%	69%	72%	72%
$\overline{CR}_p$	76%	82%	82%	1.14	1.17	1.17	.99	1.03	1.09
$CR*$	1.04	1.12	1.19	5.2	5.2	5.2	2.0	2.0	2.1
$\overline{STF}_s$	18.8	18.8	19.4	5.7	6.4	6.4	2.5	2.7	2.7
$\overline{STF}_p$	34.0	38.3	38.3	.91	.81	.81	.80	.74	.78
$STF*$	.55	.49	.51						
Adjustment 1: $M/CR* = M*$	13.6	12.6	12.8	34.3	33.4	39.1	43.4	41.7	37.9
Adjustment 2: $M*(STF*) = M**$	7.5	6.2	6.5	31.2	27	31.7	34.7	30.9	29.6

S_s = recommended man years (sample)

$\overline{M}_s$ = average recommended man years (sample).

P_s = unadjusted new man years (total population × $\overline{M}_s$)

$\overline{CR}_s$ = average sample compliance rate

$\overline{CR}_p$ = average population compliance rate

$\overline{STF}_s$ = average staff (sample)

$CR*$ = compliance adjustment index: $\overline{CR}_p/\overline{CR}_s$

$STF*$ = staff adjustment index: $\overline{STF}_s/\overline{STF}_p$

$\overline{STF}_p$ = average staff (population)

$M*$ = man years adjusted for compliance rates

$M**$ = man years adjusted for compliance rates and staffing levels

**Appendix E:
Comparative Personnel
Compliance Costs,
Methods A-C[a]**

[a]Analysis performed by Correctional Economics Center, 1975.

Method	Variables	Type 2 Man Years	Type 2 Costs	Type 3 Man Years	Type 3 Costs	Type 4 Man Years	Type 4 Costs	Total Types 2-4
A[a]	Additional man years and cost recommendations: sample jails	10.4	$ 128,381	17.9	$ 189,259	16.4	$174,861	
	Additional man years and cost estimates: population	7.5	74,573	31.2	296,306	34.7	312,890	
		17.9	$ 202,954	49.1	$ 485,565	51.1	$487,751	
	Current man years and costs	192.5	1,967,795	104.5	1,058,616	42.5	371,048	$1,176,270
	Total man years and costs	210.4	$2,170,749	153.6	$1,536,833	93.6	$868,527	$4,576,109
B[a]	Additional man years and cost recommendations: sample jails	10.4	$ 128,381	17.9	$ 189,259	16.4	$ 174,861	
	Additional man years and cost estimates: population	6.2	65,348	27	256,419	30.9	278,625	
	Additional man years and cost recommendations: extended sample	10.1	83,335	23.8	240,758	25.1	208,588	
		26.7	$ 277,064	68.7	$ 686,436	72.4	$ 662,074	
	Current man years and costs	192.5	1,967,795	104.5	1,051,268	42.5	380,776	$1,625,574
	Total man years and costs	219.2	$2,244,859	173.2	$1,737,704	114.9	$1,042,850	$4,925,413
C[b]	Additional man years and cost recommendations: sample jails	20.5	$ 211,716	41.6	$ 430,017	41.5	$ 383,449	
	Additional man years and cost estimates: population	6.5	68,510	31.7	291,989	29.6	276,286	
		27.0	$ 280,226	73.3	$ 722,006	71.1	$ 659,735	
	Current man years and costs	192.5	1,967,795	104.5	1,051,268	42.5	380,776	$1,661,967
	Total man years and costs	219.5	$2,248,021	177.8	$1,780,623	113.6	$1,030,783	$5,059,427

aSample = 14.
bSample = 22.

Appendix F:
Capital Cost Analysis

Cost Center Function	Capital Components						Total			Percent of		
	Basic		Special Equipment		Mechan./Electric					Grand Total Jail[b] Costs	Sub-total Jail[b] Costs	Jail Space
	Subtotal Cost	Cost/ Sq Ft	Subtotal Cost	Cost/ Sq Ft	Subtotal Cost	Cost/ Sq Ft	Sq Ft	Cost	Cost/ Sq Ft			
A. Jail administration and intake	$73,350	$30.00	$79,500	$ 32.52	$24,450	$10.00	2,445	$177,300	$ 72.52	10.52	12.92	13.35
1. Supervision and control ctr.	10,050	30.00	50,000	149.25	3,350	10.00	335	63,400	189.25			
2. Booking, storage, copying, waiting	12,900	30.00	10,000	23.26	4,300	10.00	430	27,200	63.26			
3. Holding cell	5,250	30.00	4,200	24.00	1,750	10.00	175	11,200	64.00			
4. Safety cell	2,400	30.00	3,800	47.50	800	10.00	80	7,000	87.50			
5. Public toilet	1,500	30.00	2,000	40.00	500	10.00	50	4,000	80.00			
6. Personal property storage	7,050	30.00	3,500	14.89	2,350	10.00	235	10,900	46.38			
7. Search, shower, ident.	9,750	30.00	3,500	10.77	3,250	10.00	325	16,500	50.77			
8. Interview	4,200	30.00	0	0	1,400	10.00	140	5,600	40.00			
9. Release area	1,500	30.00	500	10.00	500	10.00	50	2,500	50.00			
10. Female booking, storage, search	6,750	30.00	4,000	17.78	2,250	10.00	225	13,000	57.78			
11. Matron's office	7,500	30.00	0	0	2,500	10.00	250	10,000	40.00			
12. Files storage	4,500	30.00	0	0	1,500	10.00	150	6,000	40.00			
B. Medical and isolation areas	9,300	30.00	7,434	23.98	4,650	15.00	310	21,384	68.98	1.29	1.56	1.69
1. Screening and exam room	4,500	30.00	2,500	16.67	2,250	15.00	150	9,250	61.67			
2. Two isolation cells	4,800	30.00	4,934	30.84	2,400	15.00	160	12,134	75.84			

147

C. *Visiting areas*	$36,810	$30.00	$7,625	$ 6.21	$12,270	$10.00	1,227	$ 56,705	$ 46.21	3.36	4.13	6.70
1. Counter and waiting	6,000	30.00	2,000	10.00	2,000	10.00	200	10,000	50.00			
2. Professional visiting	7,440	30.00	1,500	6.05	2,480	10.00	248	11,420	46.05			
3. Social visiting/booths	16,170	30.00	4,125	7.65	5,390	10.00	539	25,685	47.65			
4. Social visiting/family	7,200	30.00	0	0	2,400	10.00	240	9,600	40.00			
D. *Food service*	51,098	30.00	87,800	51.57	17,030	10.00	1,703	155,920	91.58	9.25	11.36	9.30
1. Kitchen and dishwashing	34,950	30.00	85,000	72.96	11,650	10.00	1,165	131,600	112.96			
2. Ready storage, freezer	4,350	30.00	0	0	1,450	10.00	145	5,800	40.00			
3. Dry storage	3,750	30.00	500	4.00	1,250	10.00	125	5,500	44.00			
4. Locker room for workers	1,500	30.00	800	16.00	500	10.00	50	2,800	56.00			
5. Kitchen office	4,400	30.00	0	0	1,480	10.00	148	5,920	40.00			
6. Staff lavatories (2)	2,100	30.00	1,500	21.43	700	10.00	70	4,300	61.43			
E. *Laundry facilities*	15,150	30.00	10,800	21.39	7,575	15.00	505	33,525	66.39	1.99	2.44	2.76
1. Soiled laundry storage	3,300	30.00	300	2.73	1,650	15.00	110	5,250	47.73			
2. Clean laundry storage	3,300	30.00	500	4.55	1,650	15.00	110	5,450	49.55			
3. Workroom and supplies	8,550	30.00	10,000	35.09	4,275	15.00	285	22,825	80.09			
F. *Program and activities areas*	53,340	30.00	13,700	7.71	13,700	15.00	1,778	93,710	52.71	5.56	6.83	9.71
1. Four multipurpose rooms	15,900	30.00	2,000	3.77	7,950	15.00	530	25,850	48.77			
2. Recreation room	16,800	30.00	2,000	3.57	8,400	15.00	560	27,200	48.57			
3. Library	7,500	30.00	5,000	20.00	3,750	15.00	250	16,250	65.00			
4. Library storage	1,950	30.00	1,200	18.46	975	15.00	65	4,125	63.46			

Cost Center Function	Capital Components						Sq Ft	Total		Percent of		
	Basic		Special Equipment		Mechan./Electric					Grand Total Jail[b] Costs	Sub-total Jail[b] Costs	Jail Space
	Subtotal Cost	Cost/Sq Ft	Subtotal Cost	Cost/Sq Ft	Subtotal Cost	Cost/Sq Ft		Cost	Cost/Sq Ft			
5. Barber shop	2,700	30.00	2,500	27.78	1,350	15.00	90	6,550	72.78			
6. Mattress storage	5,040	30.00	0	0	2,520	15.00	168	7,560	45.00			
7. Miscellaneous storage	3,450	30.00	1,000	8.70	1,725	15.00	115	6,175	53.70			
G. Inmate housing (pretrial)	$310,200	$30.00	$368,630	$ 35.65	$155,100	$15.00	$10,340	$833,930	$ 80.65	49.47	60.76	56.48
1. Padded cell	1,800	30.00	7,700	128.33	900	15.00	60	10,400	173.33			
2. 23 medium security	41,400	30.00	5,566	4.03	20,700	15.00	1,380	67,666	49.03			
3. Lavatory, shower (23)	17,250	30.00	10,450	18.17	8,625	15.00	575	36,325	63.17			
4. 16 maximum security	34,560	30.00	88,432	76.76	17,280	15.00	1,152	140,272	121.76			
5. Dayroom	975	30.00	50,500	51.80	14,625	15.00	975	94,375	96.80			
Subtotal pretrial	$124,260	$30.00	$162,648	$39.27	$62,130	$15.00	4,142	$349,038	$84.27	(20.70)	(25.43)	(22.62)
Inmate housing (sentenced)												
6. 17 medium	30,600	30.00	4,114	4.03	15,300	15.00	1,020	50,014	49.03			
7. 5 maximum	10,800	30.00	27,635	76.76	5,400	15.00	360	43,835	121.76			
8. 21 minimum	37,800	30.00	5,082	4.03	18,900	15.00	1,260	61,782	49.03			
9. Dayroom	32,250	30.00	50,500	46.98	16,125	15.00	1,075	98,875	91.98			
10. Lavatory shower (min/med)	28,500	30.00	13,750	14.47	14,250	15.00	950	56,500	59.47			
Subtotal sentenced	$139,950	$30.00	$101,081	$21.67	$69,975	$15.00	4,665	$311,006	$66.67	(18.45)	(22.66)	(25.48)

Inmate housing (females)

11. 2 medium (pretrial)	$ 3,600	$30.00	$ 490	$ 4.08	$1,800	$15.00	120	$ 5,890	$ 49.08			
12. 5 maximum (pretrial)	10,800	30.00	27,635	76.76	5,400	15.00	360	43,835	121.76			
13. 2 isolation	4,320	30.00	11,054	76.76	2,160	15.00	144	17,534	121.76			
14. Dayroom (pretrial)	6,750	30.00	26,850	119.33	3,375	15.00	225	36,975	164.33			
15. Lavatory shower (medium)	1,500	30.00	3,225	64.50	750	15.00	50	5,475	109.50			
16. 4 work release	7,200	30.00	968	4.03	3,600	15.00	240	11,768	49.03			
17. 2 isolation	4,320	30.00	11,054	76.76	2,160	15.00	144	17,534	121.76			
18. Dayroom (sentenced)	4,500	30.00	20,400	136.00	2,250	15.00	150	27,150	18.00			
19. Lavatory shower (work rel.)	3,000	30.00	3,225	32.25	1,500	15.00	100	7,725	77.25			
Subtotal female	$19,020	$30.00	$135,647	$56.23	$9,510	$15.00	1,533	$173,886	$101.23	(10.31)	(12.67)	(8.37)
Subtotal, all functions	$549,240	$30.00	$575,489	$31.43	$247,745	$13.53	$18,308	$1,372,474	$74.97			
Nonassignable space	192,240	30.00	25,000	3.90	96,120	15.00	6,408	313,360	48.90	18.59	22.83	18.62
Grand total	$741,480	$30.00	$600,489	$24.30	$343,865	$13.91	$24,716	$1,685,834	$68.21			

Source: Carl Easters, "Architectural Cost Analysis, Projected Detention Facility for Thurston County Washington"; memorandum dated 13 November 1975.

aNote: Population = 1100.

bGrand total jail costs include "nonassignable space"; subtotal excludes "nonassignable."

Appendix G:
Alternative
Efficiency-Rating
Scales[a]

[a]Analysis performed by Correctional Economics Center, 1975.

Jail No.	C_1	C_2	C_3	R_1	R_2	$Q_1 = C_1/R_1$	$Q_2 = C_1/R_2$	$Q_3 = C_2/R_1$	$Q_4 = C_2/R_2$	$Q_5 = C_3/R_1$	$Q_6 = C_3/R_2$
1-1	198	398	98	18.79	12.92	10.53	15.32	21.18	30.80	5.21	7.58
2-1	184	376	88	16.47	17.18	11.17	10.71	22.82	21.88	5.34	5.12
2-2	174	356	83	5.55	5.41	31.35	32.16	64.14	65.80	15.95	15.34
2-3	174	354	84	29.21	26.79	5.95	6.49	11.83	13.21	2.87	3.13
2-4	171	355	79	11.85	9.36	14.43	18.27	29.95	37.92	6.66	8.44
2-5	155	325	70	13.03	15.42	11.89	10.05	24.94	21.07	5.37	4.53
2-6	175	365	80	15.83	14.88	11.05	11.76	23.05	24.52	5.05	5.37
2-7	137	296	65	6.64	7.54	20.63	18.16	44.57	39.25	9.78	8.62
3-1	185	373	91	14.64	11.43	12.63	16.18	25.47	32.63	6.21	7.96
3-2	179	355	91	8.33	8.78	21.48	20.38	42.62	40.43	10.92	10.36
3-3	177	361	85	12.45	18.32	14.21	9.66	28.99	19.70	6.82	4.63
3-4	186	374	92	10.58	10.80	17.58	17.22	35.35	34.62	8.69	8.76
3-5	180	370	85	12.70	12.70	14.17	14.17	29.13	29.13	6.69	6.69
3-6	183	375	87	12.84	13.62	14.25	13.93	29.20	27.53	6.77	6.38
3-7	174	358	82	11.37	12.82	15.30	13.57	31.48	27.92	7.21	6.39
3-8	166	338	80	12.70	11.80	13.07	14.06	26.61	28.64	6.29	6.77
3-9	164	332	80	11.55	10.62	14.20	15.44	28.74	31.26	6.92	7.53
3-10	171	353	80	13.58	13.58	12.59	12.59	25.99	25.99	5.89	5.89
3-11	170	348	81	4.57	4.42	37.20	38.46	76.14	78.73	17.72	18.32
3-12	166	348	75	14.78	15.24	11.23	10.89	23.54	22.83	5.07	4.92
3-13	161	333	75	9.42	11.76	17.09	13.69	35.35	28.31	7.96	6.37
3-14	152	316	70	3.37	4.21	45.10	36.10	93.76	75.06	20.77	16.39
3-15	162	334	76	55.06	51.15	2.94	3.16	6.07	6.52	1.38	1.48

3-16	163	333	78	7.26	6.03	22.45	27.03	45.86	55.22	10.74	12.93
3-17	163	329	80	19.89	18.50	8.19	8.81	16.54	17.78	4.02	4.32
3-18	155	319	73	10.91	9.96	14.20	15.56	29.23	32.03	6.69	7.32
3-19	124	262	55	12.25	10.39	10.12	11.93	21.38	25.21	4.48	5.29
4-1	185	375	90	23.96	26.04	7.72	7.10	15.65	14.40	3.78	3.45
4-2	185	371	92	14.17	12.19	13.05	15.17	26.18	30.43	6.49	7.54
4-3	177	367	82	58.45	58.45	3.03	3.03	62.78	62.78	1.40	1.40
4-4	181	371	86	19.15	16.20	9.45	11.17	19.37	22.90	4.49	5.30
4-5	165	343	76	6.87	7.60	24.01	21.71	49.92	45.13	11.06	10.00
4-6	173	359	80	7.32	8.70	23.63	19.88	49.04	41.26	10.92	9.19
4-7	180	370	85	10.94	10.74	16.45	16.75	33.82	34.45	7.76	7.91
4-8	172	362	77	31.44	30.12	5.47	5.71	11.51	12.02	2.44	2.55
4-9	173	357	81	15.17	12.02	11.40	14.39	23.53	29.70	5.33	9.75
4-10	168	342	81	51.60	54.39	3.25	3.09	6.62	6.29	1.56	1.48
4-11	151	309	72	19.61	17.54	7.70	8.61	15.75	17.61	3.67	4.10
4-12	155	315	75	11.07	13.12	14.00	11.81	28.45	24.00	6.77	5.71
4-13	152	320	68	62.39	68.86	2.44	2.20	5.12	4.64	1.08	.78
4-14	144	292	73	38.72	41.49	3.71	3.47	7.54	7.03	1.88	1.75
4-15	156	320	74	8.87	10.79	17.58	14.45	36.07	29.65	8.34	6.85
4-16	158	332	71	6.05	6.46	26.11	24.45	54.87	51.39	11.73	10.99
4-17	146	312	63	7.44	8.30	19.62	17.59	41.93	37.59	8.46	7.59
4-18	—	—	—	10.00	10.69	—	—	—	—	—	—
Total	7370	15,153	3489	778.84	779.84	643.62	634.83	1382.08	1375.26	304.64	303.17
Average	167.5	344.38	79.29	17.31	17.32	14.63	14.43	31.41	31.25	6.92	6.89

Bibliography

Books

Abbot, Edith. *The One Hundred and One County Jails of Illinois and Why They Ought to Be Abolished.* Chicago: Juvenile Protective Association of Chicago, 1916.

Burns, Henry, Jr. *Origin and Development of Jails in America.* Carbondale, Ill.: Center for the Study of Crime and Delinquency, n.d.

Dalton, Michael. *County Justice.* London: John Walthoe, 1715.

Fishman, Joseph. *Crucibles of Crime.* New York: Cosmopolis Press, 1923.

Hoffer, Frank; Martin, Delbert; and House, Floyd. *The Jails of Virginia.* New York: Appleton-Century, 1933.

Jordan, P.D. "The Close and Stinking Jail." *Frontier Law and Order: Ten Essays.* Lincoln, Neb.: University of Nebraska Press, 1970.

Lewis, Orlando. *The Development of Prison Customs, 1776-1845.* Reprint Series in Criminology, Law Enforcement and Social Problems, no. 1. Montclair, N.J.: Patterson Smith, 1967.

Robinson, Lewis. *Jails: Care and Treatment of Misdemeanant Prisoners in the United States.* Philadelphia: J.C. Winston, 1944.

_____. *Penology in the United States.* Philadelphia: J.C. Winston, 1923.

Rothman, David. *The Discovery of the Asylum: Social Order and Disorder in the New Republic.* Boston: Little, Brown, 1971.

Spencer, H. Francis. *Confessions of a Jailer.* Long Beach, Calif.: H. Francis Spencer, 1914.

Webb, Sidney, and Webb, Beatrice. *English Prisons Under Local Government.* Hamden, Conn.: Shoe String Press, 1963.

Government Publications

Hutcheson, Joseph C. "The Local Jail." *Proceedings of the Attorney General's Conference on Crime.* 10-13 December 1934. Washington, D.C., n.d.

Kansas Governor's Committee on Criminal Justice Administration and the Midwest Research Institute. *Standards and Goals for the Kansas Criminal Justice System.* 1975.

National Advisory Commission on Criminal Justice Standards and Goals. *Corrections.* Washington, D.C.: Government Printing Office, 1973.

National Commission on Law Observance and Enforcement. *Report on Penal Institutions: Probation and Parole.* Washington, D.C.: Government Printing Office, 1931.

U.S. Bureau of Prisons. *Jail Operations: A Training Course for Jail Officers.* Washington, D.C.: Government Printing Office, n.d.

U.S. Comptroller General. *Conditions in Local Jails Remain Inadequate Despite Federal Funding Improvements.* Washington, D.C.: General Accounting Office, 1976.

U.S. Department of Justice. Law Enforcement Assistance Administration. *Expenditure and Employment Data for the Criminal Justice System, 1974.* Washington, D.C.: Government Printing Office, 1976.

_____. *The Nation's Jails.* Washington, D.C.: Government Printing Office, 1975.

U.S. President's Commission on Law Enforcement and the Administration of Justice. *Task Force Report: Corrections.* Washington, D.C.: Government Printing Office, 1967.

Washington State City and County Jail Commission. *Report to the Washington State Legislature.* 1 December 1974.

Washington State Department of Social and Health Services. Office of Adult Corrections. *Jail Inspection Report (1972) to the 43rd Legislature.* Olympia, Wash.: 1972.

Reports

American Bar Association Commission on Correctional Facilities and Services. Statewide Jail Standards and Inspection Systems Project. *Survey and Handbook on State Standards and Inspection Legislation.* Washington, D.C.: American Bar Association, 1974.

_____. *Statewide Jail Standards Legislation: Developmental Profiles in Four States.* Washington, D.C.: American Bar Association, 1975.

Block, Michael. *Cost, Scale Economies, and Other Economic Concepts.* Washington, D.C.: Correctional Economics Center, 1976.

Byers, A.G. "District Prisons Under State Control for Persons Convicted of Minor Offenses: Size, Organization and Discipline Suited to Them." *Transactions of the National Congress on Penitentiary and Reformatory Discipline.* E.C. Wines, ed. Albany: Weed Parsons, 1871. Reprint. American Correctional Association, 1970.

Correctional Economics Center. *Plan for a Cost Analysis of the Corrections Report.* Washington, D.C.: Correctional Economics Center, 1975.

Funke, Gail (as Gail S.F. Monkman). *Cost Analysis of Community Correctional Centers.* Washington, D.C.: Correctional Economics Center, 1975.

Funke, Gail S. (as Gail S.F. Monkman), and Wayson, Billy L. *Comparative Costs of State and Local Facilities.* Washington, D.C.: Correctional Economics Center, 1975.

National Sheriffs' Association. "Determining Needs for Staff." *Handbook on Jail Administration.* Washington, D.C.: National Sheriff's Association, 1974.

Singer, Neil M., and Wright, Virginia B. *Cost Analysis of Correctional Standards:*

Institutional-based Programs and Parole. Washington, D.C.: Correctional Economics Center, 1976.

Stracensky, Gary; Friel, Charles; Barrum, James; and Killinger, George. *Texas Jails—Problems and Reformation*. Criminal Justice Monograph vol. 3, no. 4. Huntsville, Tex.: Institute of Contemporary Corrections and Behavioral Science, 1971.

Thalheimer, Donald T. *Cost Analysis of Correctional Standards: Halfway Houses*. Washington, D.C.: Correctional Economics Center, 1975.

Watkins, Ann M. *Cost Analysis of Correctional Standards: Pretrial Diversion*. Washington, D.C.: Correctional Economics Center, 1975.

Articles

Dowling, Oscar. 'The Hygiene of Jails, Lock-ups and Police Stations." *Journal of the American Institute of Criminal Law and Criminology* 5 (January 1915).

Fishman, Joseph. "The American Jail: Pages from the Diary of a Prison Inspector." *Atlantic Monthly*, vol. 130 (December 1922).

Lane, Winthrop. "Uncle Sam, Jailer: A Study of the Conditions of Federal Prisoners in Kansas Jails." *Survey*, vol. 42 (1919).

Mattick, Hans W. and Aikman, Alexander B. "The Cloacal Region of American Corrections." *The Annals of The American Academy of Political and Social Science,* no. 381 (January 1969).

Mattick, Hans. "The Contemporary Jails of the United States." *Handbook of Criminology*. Daniel Glaser, ed. Chicago: Rand-McNally, 1974.

Ruggles-Brise, Sir Evelyn. "English View of the American Penal System." *Journal of the American Institute of Criminal Law and Criminology*, vol. 2, no. 3 (September 1911).

Smith, R.L. "A Quiet Revolution: Probation Subsidy." *Delinquency Prevention Reporter* (May 1971).

Unpublished Reports, Memoranda, and Interviews

Easters, Carl E. "Architectural Cost Analysis, Projected Detention Facility for Thurston County, Washington." November 13, 1975. "Washington State Jail Analysis: Remodeling Estimates." December, 1975. Memoranda from Bennett, Johnson, Slenes & Smith, AIA & Associates, Olympia, Wash.

Mikesell, John. "Local Jails Operating Cost and Economic Analysis: Scale Economies in Local Jail Operations." Paper presented at the Southern Economic Association, Atlanta, 15 November 1974.

Murphy, James E. Potomac Justice Institute. Riverdale, Md. Interview, November 1975.

Paulson, Dennis, and Powell, Floyd. Washington State Jail Commission, Olympia, Wash. Interviews, October-November 1975.

Ruehl, Gordon. "Eastern Washington Jail Survey Reports, I and II." 25 November 1975 and 6 December 1975. Memoranda from Walker/McGough/Foltz/Lyerla, Architects & Engineers, Spokane, Wash.

Schram, Donna; Walsh, Marilyn; and Ulberg, Cyrus. *Washington State Jail Populations 1972-75 with Projections through 1979.* Human Affairs Research Centers, Battelle Memorial Institute, November 1975.

Seattle Central Community College. *Progress Report*, 14 August 1975. Law Justice Planning Office Grant #1521.

Index

Allocation of costs. *See* Costs

Alternatives to incarceration
 community based corrections, 23
 costs of, 28
 necessity for a system-wide perspective in analysis of, 10, 22
 pretrial diversion, 7, 10, 23
 trend away from, 8

Budgeting, Accounting and Reporting
 System in Washington State
 (BARS), 41, 51-52, 131-132
Budgeting methods and usefulness in
 analysis, 40, 45

Capital costs. *See* Costs
Commissions for jail standards as a
 means for reform, 11-13
Comparability of key terms for jail
 operations, 13
Compliance rates for standards in
 Washington State, 42-44
Correctional Economics Center, 21,
 30, 35, 36, 64
Corrections Task Force of the National Advisory Commission of
 Criminal Justice Standards and
 Goals, 5, 21, 22, 26
 regionalization concept, 15
 training recommendations of, 52
Costs
 allocation of, 28-30
 allocation of direct costs within
  jails, 106
 allocation of new capital costs over
  time, 74n
 alternatives to incarceration costs,
  28
 architectural design plans for capital
  standards implementation, 51,
  63-65
 assessing cost implications of standards. *See* Standards (Jail)
 average daily cost (current operating costs) definition, 39

capital costs, failure to allocate
 properly, 26 (*see also* Costs:
 developing capital standards
 implementation costs methodology; estimating standards implementation costs, new and remodeled)
categorization of standards by cost
 center, 38, 39, 111-130
cost effectiveness as a function of
 jail size, 14, 16 (*see also* Economies of scale)
definitions of, 30
definitions of in Washington State
 Study, 39
developing capital standards implementation costs methodology,
 63-74
developing non-capital standards
 implementation costs methodology, 51-62 (*see also* Estimating
 implementation costs for specific
 non-capital standards groups
estimating standards' implementation costs, 51-75; of capital
 (new), 65-70; of capital (remodeled), 70-74, 145-150; of
 educational, counseling and
 training services, 62; of health
 services, 60-62; of personnel,
 55-58, 141-144; of supplies
 (office and operating—includes
 food), 58, 60
excluded, 40
external, 40
failure to allocate capital costs,
 26-27
hidden, 27
impact of in Washington State
 Study, 41-42, 44, 51
joint products, 27-29
operating costs in Washington State,
 1974, 45-46
opportunity costs of jail processes,
 105

159

About the Authors

Billy L. Wayson is Director of the Correctional Economics Center. For the last three years he has initiated and coordinated research on the economics of medical experimentation on prisoners, pretrial diversion, probation, halfway houses, women offenders, and purchase-of-service contracting. His prior experience in operating agencies included duties in management analysis, planning, performance measurement, and budgeting. He has served as Special Assistant to the Director of the United States Bureau of Prisons, Deputy Director of the National Conference on Criminal Justice Standards and Goals (1973), Staff Associate to the Corrections Task Force of the National Advisory Commission on Criminal Justice Standards and Goals (1972), and as Co-Director of the National Conference on Corrections (1971). In addition, he has served on advisory boards to the Council of State Governments, Center for Policy Studies, and Mathematica, Inc., for projects concerning prison industries, the future of corrections, and information needs of state and local officials.

Gail S. Funke has been Assistant Director (as Gail S.F. Monkman) of the Correctional Economics Center since its inception. An economist by profession, she received the B.A. from Rutgers University, the M.A. from Hunter College, and is currently completing her doctoral work at the City University of New York. Since coming to the Center, she has assisted in its exploration of the economic implications of correctional decision making. Her publications and papers (as Gail S.F. Monkman) include: *Cost Analysis of Community Corrections Centers–A Case Study: Indiana* (Correctional Economics Center, 1975); *Comparative Costs of State and Local Facilities* (with Billy L. Wayson) (Correctional Economics Center, 1975); "The Economics of Crime and Community," *Law in American Society*, (February 1975); and "The Economic Future of Corrections," paper presented before the Southern States Correctional Association, June 1976.

Sally F. Familton received the M.S. in public policy analysis from Averell Harriman College of Urban and Policy Sciences, State University of New York at Stony Brook. She has worked previously with the Correctional Economics Center on cost analyses of a juvenile diversion program and the Washington State Jail Standards Implementation project. Her interests include improving the accuracy of data used in decision making, and developing evaluation methodologies applicable to policy questions, particularly from an economic perspective.

Peter B. Meyer is Associate Professor of Economic Planning in the Division of Community Development at the Pennsylvania State University. Professor Meyer is the author of numerous articles in the field of social policy choice and planning, including *Drug Experiments on Prisoners* (Lexington Books, 1976), and he directs his research toward issues contributing to the development of a more democratic economic and social system in the United States.

Soc
HV
9471
L6

DATE DUE

JAN 21 1979	APR 17 198
CT APR 20 1989	
JUN 1989	
JUL 11 1989	
MAR 05 1991	